Quirky
GLOUCESTER

PAUL JAMES

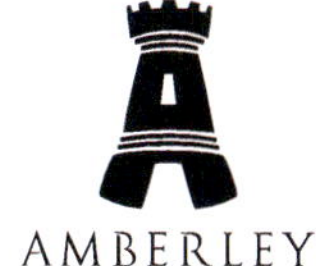

AMBERLEY

First published 2025

Amberley Publishing
The Hill, Stroud
Gloucestershire, GL5 4EP

www.amberley-books.com

British Library Cataloguing in Publication Data.
A catalogue record for this book is available from the British Library.

ISBN 978 1 3981 2307 6 (paperback)
ISBN 978 1 3981 2308 3 (ebook)

Typesetting by SJmagic DESIGN SERVICES, India.
Printed in Great Britain.

Appointed GPSR EU Representative:
Easy Access System Europe Oü, 16879218
Address: Mustamäe tee 50, 10621, Tallinn, Estonia
Contact Details: gpsr.requests@easproject.com, +358 40 500 3575

Contents

Introduction

As a resident of Gloucester for over fifty years, with twenty-four of those as a city councillor and over twelve as Leader of the Council, I probably know Gloucester's quirks better than most. Someone wrote to me as Leader of the Council asking why the city didn't make more of Gloucester's most famous son, Button Gwinnett. At the time I had no idea who he was! I had no clue that the second signatory to the US Declaration of Independence had been born just outside Gloucester and had been baptised, had lived and was educated within the city. Since then I've done my best to spread knowledge of this story, including mentioning it in more detail in this book.

On another occasion I received a letter asking why there wasn't more in the city commemorating the life of Aethelflaed, the Saxon Warrior Queen and Lady of the Mercians, given her influence on Gloucester and on England as we know it today. It's a fair point. She founded St Oswald's Priory and has a plaque there, although perhaps not in the most prominent place. What is believed to be her gravestone is on display at the Museum of Gloucester. There was talk of commissioning a statue of Aethelflaed but that came to nothing, largely because finding the money for something like this is rarely easy. She is buried at St Oswald's Priory, but we don't actually know exactly where on the site she is. Maybe one day her body will be found and it will cause a media storm, just like the discovery of Richard III in a Leicester car park did in 2012.

Over the years, I've been involved in a fair few of Gloucester's quirky traditions. As Sheriff of Gloucester, I reintroduced the Sheriff's Assize of Ale in 2003 and I'm a proud member of the Court Leet of Barton St Mary which oversees the election (if that's the right word) of the Mock Mayor of Barton. During my life in the city, I've come to know many of the city's colourful characters.

Despite its many centuries of history and the important part it has played in the nation's story, Gloucester as a city doesn't take itself too seriously – and that's part of its charm. Although the city lost many fine buildings during the large-scale redevelopment of the 1960s and 1970s (much of which as a city we now regret) there are still plenty of fine, and quirky, buildings left and this book highlights a few of the best examples.

Gloucester isn't particularly known for its public art, and has been described by some (I think unfairly) as a cultural desert, but this book takes a look at some of the pieces of art dotted around the city centre. Public art is subjective and, inevitably, opinions vary. Nonetheless, many of these pieces have interesting stories behind them and make more sense when you know what the story is.

As a lifelong Gloucester Rugby fan and season ticket holder for around forty years, I've seen the passion of the club's supporters, which can be demonstrated at times in some quirky ways!

I hope you enjoy reading this book, that it teaches you some facts about the city that you didn't know before and that, once you've read it, you may see Gloucester in a different light.

Food and Drink

Gloucester Lager

If you had to associate a drink with Gloucester, it would probably be a pint of Gloucester Gold, produced by the Gloucester Brewery at the city's docks. Less well known is that Gold Label (GL) cider, initially produced by Bulmers and now under the Weston's banner, was known as Gloucester Lager because of its popularity in this area. Westons revived the brand in October 2012, two years after it had been discontinued by Bulmers.

Gloucester Cakes

On the sweet side, the city is known for its dripping cakes, known as 'Gloucester Drips' and 'Lardy Cakes'. Bakers such as Featherstones, who had shops in Eastgate Street and Bell Walk and a bakery on London Road, were famous for them. The secret to making them was, apparently, using lard from Gloucester Old Spot pigs – although that might be a myth! Few, if any, bakeries in the city sell them any longer, but at the time of writing, Oakdens, a bakery in Alvington in the Forest of Dean still makes them.

An old recipe for the Gloucester Tart was included in the book *Gloucester – A Miscellany* compiled by Julia Skinner. An attempt was made to bring back the tart, which is similar to a Bakewell Tart, into popular circulation in 2014 when the author of this book was Leader of Gloucester City Council. It didn't catch on here, but more recently it has been made to celebrate Gloucester Day 2023 in Gloucester County, Virginia, in the USA! Chris Thomas, known as the 'Library Chef', made the tart after seeking advice from Jordan Cox, who appeared on the *Great British Bake Off*, and Irish chef and baking expert Gemma Stafford. Chris's exploits can be seen on The Library Kitchen's YouTube channel.

Gloucester Tart Recipe
Ingredients:
175g/6oz-Shortcrust Pastry
50g/2oz-Butter or Margarine
50g/2oz-Caster Sugar
1-Egg
1tsp-Almond Extract
50g/2oz Ground Rice (may substitute rice flour)
Raspberry Jam

Directions:

Preheat oven to 350 degrees.

Grease a patty tin.

Roll out the pastry on a lightly floured surface and cut in 2inch circles and use the circles to linc the patty tins.

Cream the sugar and butter/margarine together until light and fluffy. Beat the egg to the creamed mixture, a little at a time. Stir in the Almond Extract and Rice Flour. Mix thoroughly. This mixture is called a frangipane.

Place 1 tsp of Raspberry Jam in each patty tin. Top with a tsp of frangipane.

Bake 22–25 minutes until filling is firm and topping is lightly golden. Cool and enjoy.

Acknowledgement: The Library Kitchen

Right: A batch of Gloucester Tarts. (Gloucester County Library)

Below: Chris Thomas preparing Gloucester Tarts on Gloucester Day 2023 in Gloucester County, Virginia, with journalist Betty Wrenn Day. (Gloucester County Library)

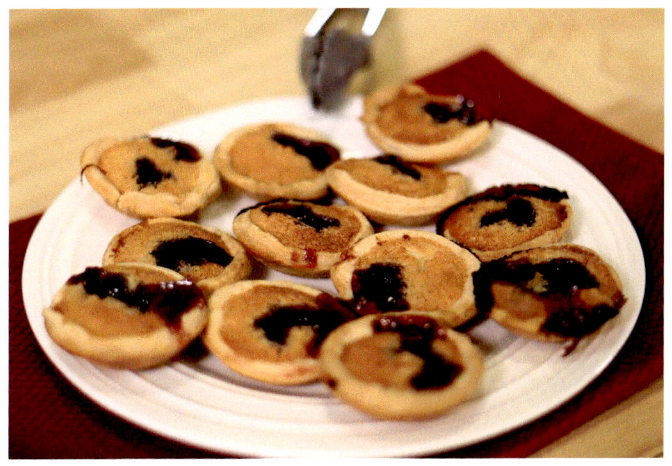

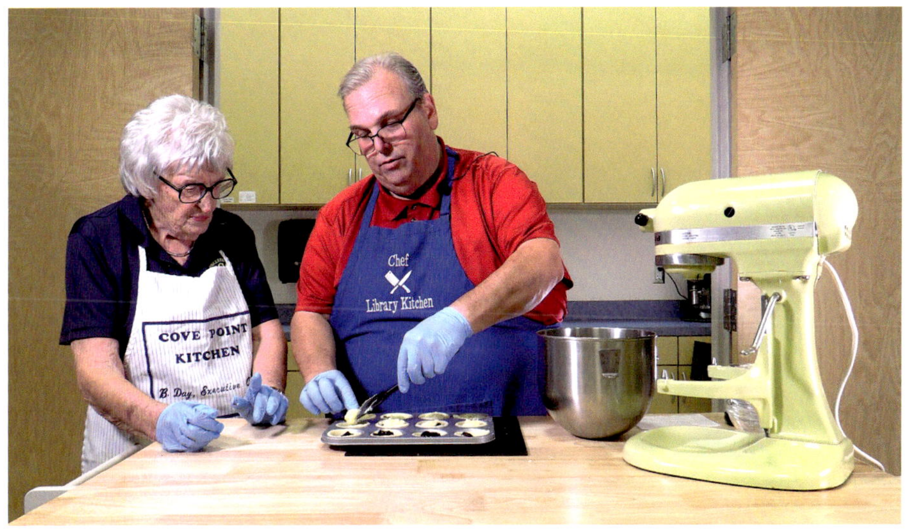

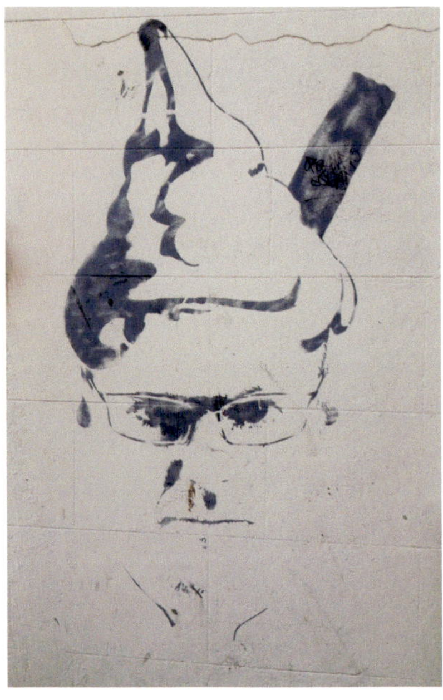

A street art image of Heston Blumenthal on a property in Cromwell Street, marking his attempt to build the world's largest ice cream in Gloucester Park.

The World's Biggest Ice Cream

Gloucester is, of course, famous for the Wall's Ice Cream factory, which at one point was the biggest in Europe. It is because of this connection that Gloucester Park was chosen by the celebrity chef Heston Blumenthal for a record attempt to make the world's biggest ice cream in 2012. It was 4 metres tall, weighed over a ton and took a month to freeze! Toppings, including sauce and hundreds and thousands, were catapulted onto the top of the creation – although most failed to stick!

The Lamprey Pie

Gloucester has been presenting a lamprey pie to the reigning monarch since the medieval era. By 1200 it had become customary for the city of Gloucester to send the English monarch a pie every year, and King John fined the city 40 marks or £26 13s 4d (equivalent to £38,000 in 2020) for failing to send a pie at Christmas. The custom of Gloucester sending the monarch a lamprey pie, decorated with gilded ornaments, at Christmas ended in 1836 when it was considered too expensive.

Lampreys were eaten by the Romans since at least the first century AD and were considered a high-status food. The food became associated with medieval Christmases, as Christmas Eve, the last day of Advent, was a fast day. They were popular with royalty – Henry I is said to have died after eating 'a surfeit of lampreys'. The lamprey pie also features in the television drama *Game of Thrones*.

The prevalence of lampreys in English rivers declined in the nineteenth century, possibly as a result of the increasing numbers of weirs installed. The lamprey is said to have vanished from the upper reaches of the Severn by the middle of the century, with a further decline apparent from 1865. It is now a protected species.

A lamprey pie is still presented by Gloucester to the monarch on special occasions. A 20-pound (9.1 kg) pie was presented at the 1953 Coronation of Elizabeth II. Although the lampreys were supplied by a Gloucester-based company, they were sourced from Grimsby. A pie was also presented at the Silver Jubilee in 1977. By the time of the 2002 Golden Jubilee no British lampreys could be sourced, and lampreys from the Great Lakes in Canada have been used for this and several subsequent occasions.

By the time of Queen Elizabeth II's Platinum Jubilee in 2022, in light of the climate emergency, it was felt unsustainable to fly lampreys from the other side of the world. It was also felt that it wouldn't be right at a time of a cost of living crisis to make a pie that wouldn't be eaten. Instead, lampreys were represented in specially coloured pastry on the crust of a pie filled with a historic Gloucestershire Pie recipe based on Old Spot pork and apple. The pie was made by the chefs at the Farmers Boy Inn at Longhope, just outside Gloucester, home of the famous Mad About Pies gourmet pie business and presented to the county's Lord Lieutenant Edward Gillespie OBE at Llanthony Secunda Priory. This venue was chosen because records show that in 1530 the Prior of Llanthony sent 'cheese, carp and baked lampreys' to King Henry VIII at Windsor. With the agreement of the Royal Household, the Lord Lieutenant agreed to pass the pie onto 'Gloucester Feed the Hungry', who used it to help those in need.

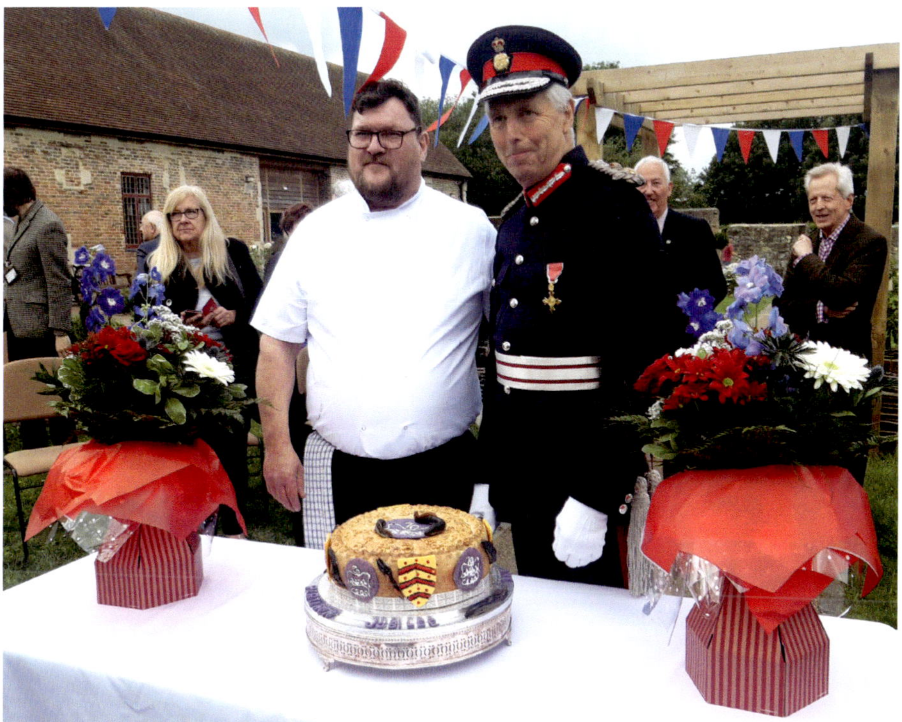

The lamprey pie being presented to Lord Lieutenant Edward Gillespie at Llanthony Secunda Priory in 2022.

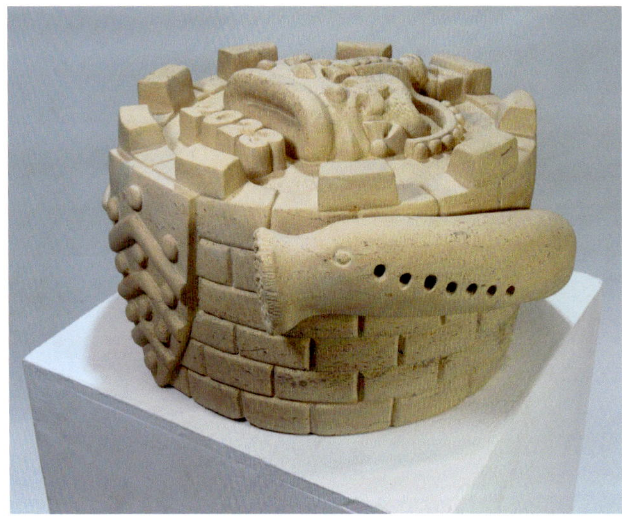

A stone-carved version of the lamprey pie which was due to be presented to King Charles III to go in the gardens at Highgrove. (Debs Harrison)

When King Charles III acceded to the throne, catering staff at The Folk of Gloucester in Westgate Street, which is run by the Gloucester Civic Trust, made a similar pie and it was again presented to HM's Lord Lieutenant and passed to Gloucester Feed the Hungry. At the time of writing, a project is underway to create a stone version of the lamprey pie, carved by local sculptor Debs Harrison, to go in the garden at King Charles' home at Highgrove, near Tetbury in Gloucestershire.

Say Cheese

Probably the most famous food associated with Gloucester is cheese – both the Single Gloucester and Double Gloucester varieties.

Gloucester is a traditional, semi-hard cheese which has been made in Gloucestershire since the sixteenth century. There are two varieties of the cheese, Single and Double. Both are traditionally made from milk from Gloucester cattle, and both types have a natural rind and a hard texture, but Single Gloucester is more crumbly, lighter in texture and lower in fat. Double Gloucester is allowed to age for longer periods than Single, and it has a stronger and more savoury flavour. It is also slightly firmer.

Manufacture of traditional Gloucester cheeses from the Gloucester cow died out in the 1950s along with most of the Gloucester cattle. However, in 1973 Charles Martell from Dymock, just outside Gloucester, managed to gather three Old Gloucester cows from the herd of fewer than fifty left in the county. A BBC TV series, *A Taste of Britain,* filmed his successful attempt to revive the tradition of farmhouse Double Gloucester that year. In 1978 Mr Martell went on to revive the lost Single Gloucester cheese. Single Gloucester cheese has Protected Designation of Origin and can only be made in Gloucestershire on farms with Gloucester cows. As of 2010 six cheese makers are producing this cheese.

The reason for the two types of Gloucester cheese being called 'Double' and 'Single' is not known. The main theories are because the creamy milk had to be skimmed twice to make the Double variety, or because cream from the morning milk was added to the evening milk, or because a Double Gloucester cheese is typically twice the height.

Charles Martell is also well known for his 'Stinking Bishop' cheese which featured in the 2005 Wallace and Gromit film *The Curse of the Were-Rabbit*, where Gromit uses it to revive Wallace.

On Toast

On Toast is the country's first toast bar, based on the West Quay of Gloucester Docks, which simply serves everything with toast. It has been going since 2011 and is run by former cruise ship entertainer David Purchase, who also worked as an assistant to the ex-Labour MP for Gloucester, Parmjit Dhanda. He has run the London Marathon with 'Mr Toasty' on his vest and also stood for the City Council in 2023 with 'known as Mr Toasty' on the ballot paper! The idea for a specialist toast-themed takeaway came from a conversation with a friend while out canvassing.

On Toast serves typical toasted sandwiches and your usual jam on toast or cheese on toast. But they also offer more adventurous options including a Mars bar or Banoffee toastie or Cadbury's Creme Egg toastie, or even a seasonal Christmas Feast deep-filled toastie!

Their 'Paddington Toastie' is made of orange marmalade, red onion & Brie. The Chocoholic Delight contains two Mars bars and two Snickers bars on a bed of Nutella and the Meat Feast is packed with BBQ chicken, cheese, pepperoni, ham and bacon.

Other sophisticated options are available, inspired by different countries around the world including Greece, Canada and America.

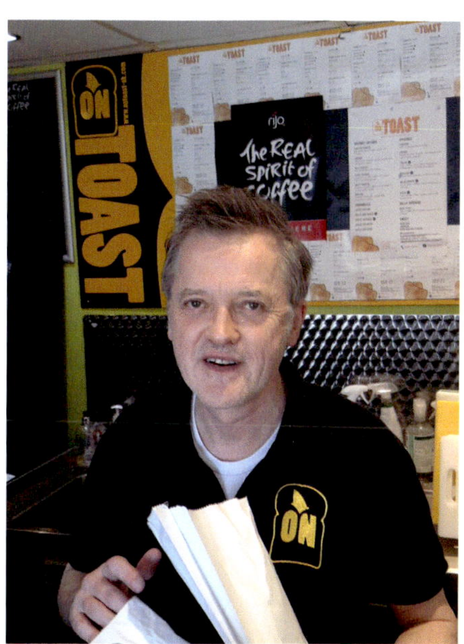

David Purchase in his 'On Toast' cafe at the Docks.

Customs and Traditions

Cheese-rolling

Cheese-rolling is a world-famous annual event held on the spring bank holiday at Cooper's Hill at Brockworth, just outside Gloucester. Competitors race down the 200-yard-long hill, with a slope of around 50 per cent, chasing a 3–4kg wheel of Double Gloucester cheese. The event has a long tradition going back at least 200 years, but most probably much longer. People from across the world take part.

The first competitor over the finish line at the bottom of the hill wins the cheese. Multiple races are held during the day, with separate events for men and women. Chris Anderson from Brockworth has won a record twenty-three races. Large crowds gather to watch the event and it has been viewed millions of times on YouTube.

The Sheriff's Assize of Ale

The Sheriff's Assize of Ale raises funds for the city's civic charities and dates back to medieval times when the sheriff was responsible for ensuring the ale on sale in the city was of palatable quality.

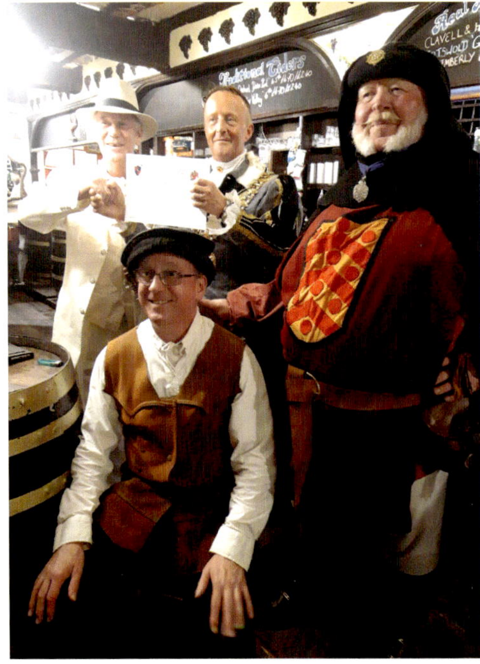

A certificate being presented to Café René by Sheriff Justin Hudson after passing the Assize of Ale test.

The sheriff, together with an army of followers dressed in medieval clothing, tours the pubs in the city's historic core collecting cash for charity and carrying out a slightly bizarre ritual involving a wooden stool, someone dressed in leather breeches and an egg timer. The sheriff has an 'Ale Conner', whose job is to sit on a wooden stool, on which a small amount of ale has been poured, wearing a pair of leather trousers.

If after three minutes the trousers stick to the stool, the ale does not pass the test. Conversely if the Ale Conner can move freely at the end of the three minutes, it does pass. The tradition was reintroduced in 2003 by the author during his year as Sheriff of Gloucester and has taken place every year since, other than during the COVID-19 pandemic. The author continues to organise the event with Town Crier Alan Myatt, with a host of city councillors and other local 'characters' taking part. The event has raised over £20,000 for the civic charities since it was introduced.

The Mock Mayor of Barton

The Mayor of Barton is a 'mock' mayor, one of only a few left in England, and probably unique in that it is an urban office rather than one attached to a rural community. It all started when Charles II returned to the throne. He didn't like Gloucester very much, because of what happened in the Civil War. After the

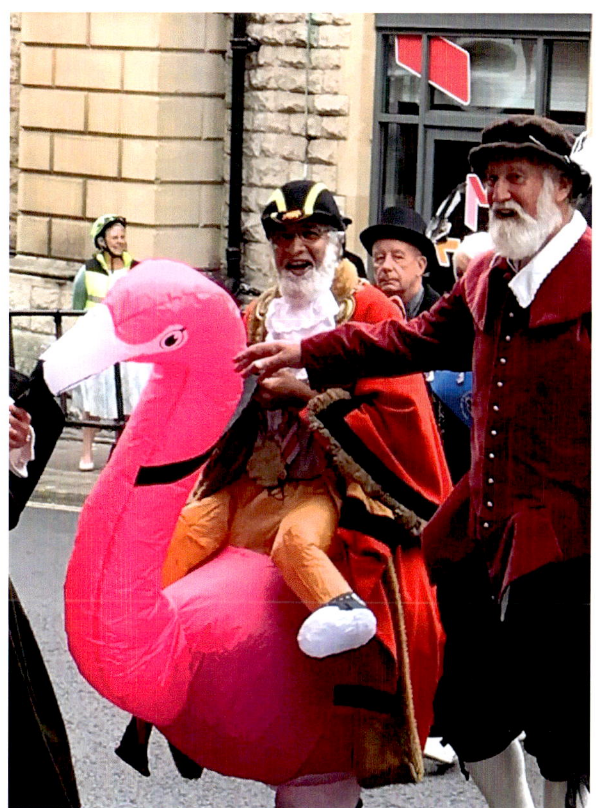

Said Hansdot as Mayor of Barton being transported on a pink inflatable flamingo.

Restoration, Charles took his revenge in various ways, knocking down the city walls, and severely reducing the city boundaries. This left the Barton area outside the city. The residents were not amused and decided that if they couldn't defer to the Mayor of Gloucester, then they'd invent their own, simply to poke fun at Gloucester's official powers that be. The tradition was revived by a group of local people, led by shopkeeper Jean George, in the mid-1980s and is now combined with Gloucester Day, which celebrates the lifting of the Siege of Gloucester.

A procession leads the mock mayor, usually travelling in a whacky form of transport (which have included a skip, a wheelie bin and an inflatable flamingo!), to meet the real mayor, where gifts (and sometimes the odd jibe) are exchanged. During the year, the Mock Mayor of Barton is asked to present prizes, open events and generally work on behalf of the community.

Freemen of the City

Freeman of Gloucester historically have had certain rights and privileges within the city, including being able to sit on the Common Council of the City,

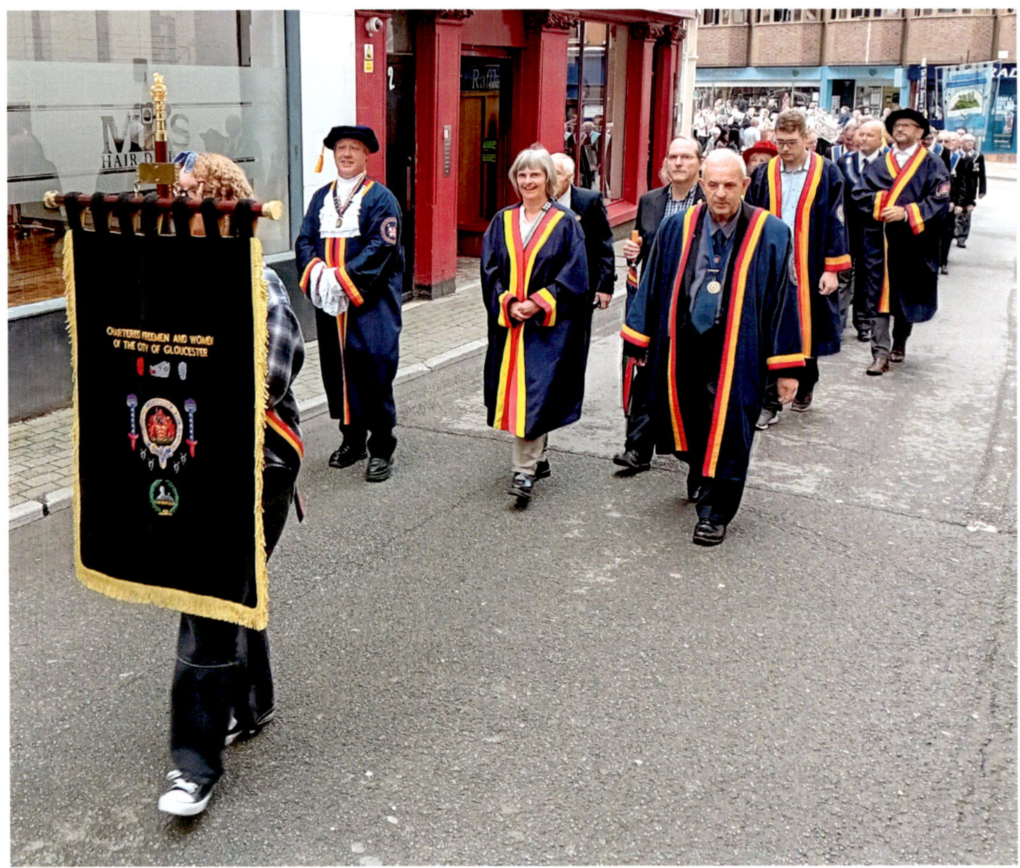

Freemen of Gloucester processing through the city centre. (Lee Hensley)

preferential trading rights, freedom from paying local tolls, grazing rights in the common meadows along the bank of the River Severn and reserved places in almshouses and schools.

By the nineteenth century the advantages of becoming a freeman had declined in importance but it did give extra status in Gloucester. There are four qualifications for admission as a freeman of the city: inherited upon reaching the age of twenty-one, completing a seven-year apprenticeship, by fine or payment or at the gift of the mayor and council. The latter is normally granted to distinguished figures, which have included the Duke of Gloucester, the Duke of Beaufort, the three Gloucester Rugby players in the 2003 World Cup-winning squad (Phil Vickery, Trevor Woodman and Andy Gomarsall) and others who have done a lot for the city, such as Town Crier Alan Myatt and former Gloucester Civic Trust chairman Robin Morris.

Freemen have traditionally been admitted through the male line. It need not be a continuous one, it being possible to inherit through a paternal grandfather, great-grandfather or even earlier. The law changed in 2009 by an Act of Parliament that allowed daughters of Freemen to take up the honour. The first in Gloucester were enrolled in 2010. In March 2025, Sheila Tuckey claimed the freedom at the age of 101 – a record in all guilds in the country. Admission through apprenticeship was last recorded in 1863.

At the last count there were over 350 registered Freemen, mostly resident within Gloucestershire and surrounding areas with the remainder scattered all over the world. The number has swelled in recent years thanks to an increase in females taking up the Freedom.

In 1996 the Freemen designed robes which are worn on special occasions such as Gloucester Day. On Gloucester Day in 2016, for the first time in centuries, Freemen of the City exercised their right to drive sheep over The Cross in the city centre. The idea came from Town Crier Alan Myatt, who had been made a freeman the previous year. The sheep came from the City Farm in Tredworth.

The Gloucester Mummers

On Boxing Day every year at midday, the Gloucester City Mummers Play is performed outside Gloucester Cathedral, after some morris dancing from various local groups. It has become a very popular tradition and draws a large crowd.

Mummers plays have been performed since the eighteenth century and were performed by farmers or builders during the Christmas season as a way to raise a bit of money when there was little in the way of work.

It happens because of a dedicated group of Gloucestershire folk music and folklore enthusiasts, mainly members of the Gloucester Folk Club, who decided to resurrect the 'Gloucester Mummers Play' back in the winter of 1969.

Before this revival, the play had not been performed for many years in Gloucester. Thankfully, in 1931 a Mr Todd had 'collected' the play from one of

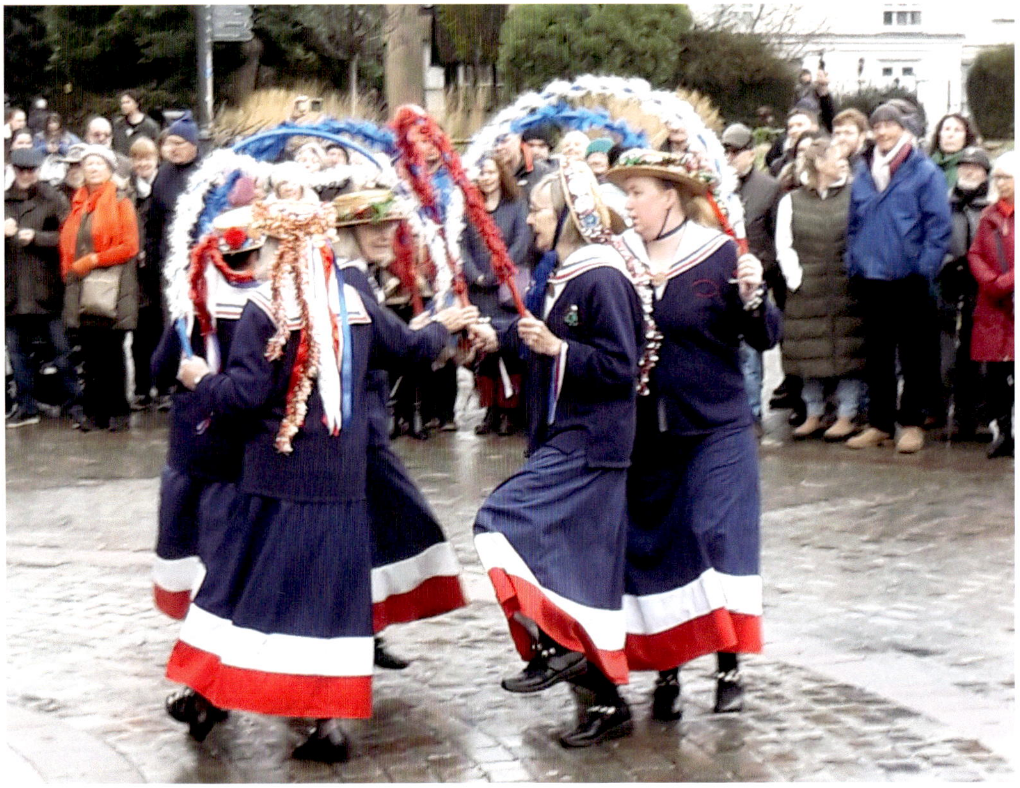

Morris dancing outside Gloucester Cathedral on Boxing Day.

the old performers, sixty-four-year-old George Blick, and so (although it hadn't been performed) it was preserved for us to enjoy to this day.

Some of the original cast were members of The Gloucestershire Morris Men but now all the cast are Gloucestershire Morris Mummers which now includes a female Old Father Christmas and characters including Bellsy Bob, Turkey Snipe (the Turkish knight) and Robin Wood.

The Severn Bore

The Severn Bore is an impressive tidal wave of water on the River Severn which works its way up the Severn Estuary over 25 miles between Awre in the Forest of Dean and Gloucester.

The spectacle is caused by the tide from the Atlantic Ocean entering the Bristol Channel and forcing its way up the Severn Estuary, filtering into a narrow channel and causing tides to rise up to 15 metres.

The wave can reach speeds of up to 13 mph and as the width of the River Severn narrows, the wave becomes upheld and produces the world-famous Severn Bore. The closest place to the centre of Gloucester to watch the Bore is from Telford's Bridge at Over, just to the west of the city.

Many surfers see the Severn Bore as one of the best river waves to surf in the world. People flock to the area in the spring and autumn to have a go at riding the waves. In 2006, Steve King set the world record for the longest surfing ride on the Severn Bore, racking up a distance of 7.6 miles. It took him 1 hour and 17 minutes.

In December 2015, there was an unworldly scene when a trio of Star Wars Stormtroopers surfed a spectacular Severn Bore from Newnham-on-Severn, 13 miles outside Gloucester, to mark the nearby Forest of Dean's role as a film location for *Star Wars*.

Apple Wassailing

Wassailing is an ancient tradition which is believed to originate from the Anglo-Saxon era. The Apple Tree Wassail involves singing a rousing blessing to apple trees to encourage them to have a healthy yield at harvest time. The word wassail is thought to come from an old Norse phrase and is loosely translated as 'be in good health'.

Wassailing is traditionally associated with Twelfth Night, but in modern times it can take place any time during December and January. The Folk of Gloucester's Apple Tree Wassail keeps alive a tradition that's been taking place in Gloucestershire's orchards for hundreds of years, with a procession, log fire, apple tree blessing and wassail song.

One of the trees at The Folk is an Ashmead Kernel tree, which is unique to Gloucester and produces a traditional russet apple with a pear-like flavour that isn't found in shops.

Animals

Lucky, the Litter-picking Dog

A dog from Gloucester called Lucky made it into the *Daily Mail* in 2010 after his owner trained him to pick up litter and drop it into the nearest bin. The three-year-old Kelpie-Doberman cross was taught to identify different types of rubbish by owner William Keating, a former builder.

He collected cans, crisp packets and plastic bottles from parks near his home in the city before jumping up onto his hind legs to place them into bins. However, if Lucky found a glass bottle he would bark twice so that Mr Keating could check for broken shards. Lucky and Mr Keating appeared on stage in the Civic Variety Show at the Gloucester Guildhall in 2011.

Sheep in Matson

Flocks of sheep have roamed the former council estates in the Matson area of Gloucester for decades, grazing on communal grassed areas around blocks of flats and even wandering in and out of the gardens of houses in the area.

People in the city suburb have embraced it, with a community hub in the area being named 'The Ewe Space' and sheep appearing on locally designed signs for the area.

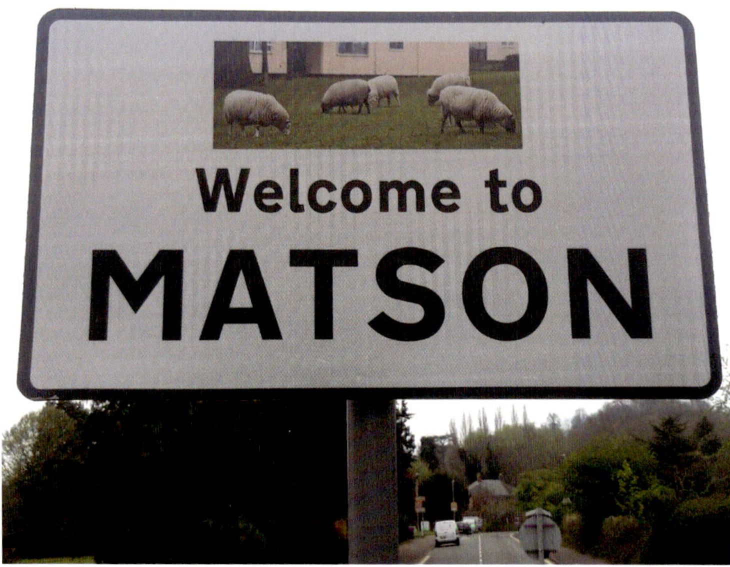

A sign on the Matson Lane roundabout celebrating the area's wandering sheep.

The Lion Tragedy

Somewhere in Gloucester cemetery is the grave of a German boy killed in the city by a lion.

The unfortunate lad was part of a lion-taming act by a performer named Madam Ella and her husband, who were appearing at the Palace Theatre in Westgate Street in the early years of the last century.

There wasn't a great deal of space at the theatre, so all the members of the act (including the lion) shared a dressing room. While Madam Ella and her husband were elsewhere in the building, the lion attacked the German boy and he sustained injuries from which he died.

The Palace Theatre was previously called the Theatre Royal. It later became Woolworths, then Texas DIY and then was home to Poundstretcher. Charles Dickens once performed a scene from *The Pickwick Papers* to a capacity audience at the theatre. The building is said to be haunted by an actress called Eliza Johnson who is said to have hanged herself after falling in love with the theatre's manager, who didn't feel the same about her.

Gloucester Old Spot Pigs

The history of the Gloucester Old Spot pig dates back to the early nineteenth century in Gloucestershire and is one of the oldest pig breeds in England. They were traditionally kept in orchards to feed on fallen fruit – hence their name 'Old Spot'. The pigs would roam freely in the orchards, consuming windfall apples and other fruits, which contributed to their unique flavour and marbling in the meat.

The breed was further developed and standardised in the late nineteenth century by breeders who aimed to improve its characteristics. They focused on traits such as the distinctive black spots on a white coat, good mothering abilities, and a docile temperament.

The Old Spot, by legend, is the pig that 'saved the city' during the Siege of Gloucester – by making so much noise that the Royalists thought there were lots of pigs and there was no danger of the Parliamentarians running out of food!

In the mid-twentieth century, however, the Gloucester Old Spot faced a decline in numbers due to changing farming practices and the rise of intensive pig farming. By the 1960s, the breed was listed as rare. However, dedicated conservation efforts by breed enthusiasts and organisations helped revive its population to what it is today.

The Gloucester Old Spot is still considered a rare breed, but its numbers have increased due to the preservation of a breed that embodies a rich agricultural heritage. The Old Spot was the inspiration for the 'Henson' pig sculpture trail around the city in 2017. Joe Henson, father of television presenter Adam, played a big part in saving rare breeds.

Gloucester Cattle

The Gloucester is one of the oldest breeds of cow and they originated in the Severn Vale and throughout Gloucestershire as early as the thirteenth century. They were valued for their meat and milk (producing cheese) and their strength. They were most popular around 1750 with the breed reaching from Devon to Essex and up to the Welsh coast but then the numbers decreased as disease, development of other breeds and arable farming increased.

In 1796 the Gloucester cow Blossom provided the first anti-smallpox serum to Sir Edward Jenner as he noticed that milkmaids were free of smallpox.

Originally formed in 1919, the Gloucester Cattle Society was revived in 1973 initially to provide for the survival of the breed. The society has been very successful and breed numbers have now grown to over 700 registered females. The cattle are again recognised for their contribution to the environment and for their superb beef and cheese quality.

The Gloucester is categorised as a rare breed by the Rare Breeds Survival Trust and its status is monitored on the Watchlist.

The Barnwood Bunnies

When a colony of wild rabbits made their home in the middle of one of the city's busiest road junctions – Wall's roundabout in Barnwood – it attracted huge media coverage, lots of visitors and became one of Gloucester's best-loved landmarks. They became known as the 'Barnwood Bunnies', with their home being labelled 'Rabbit Roundabout'.

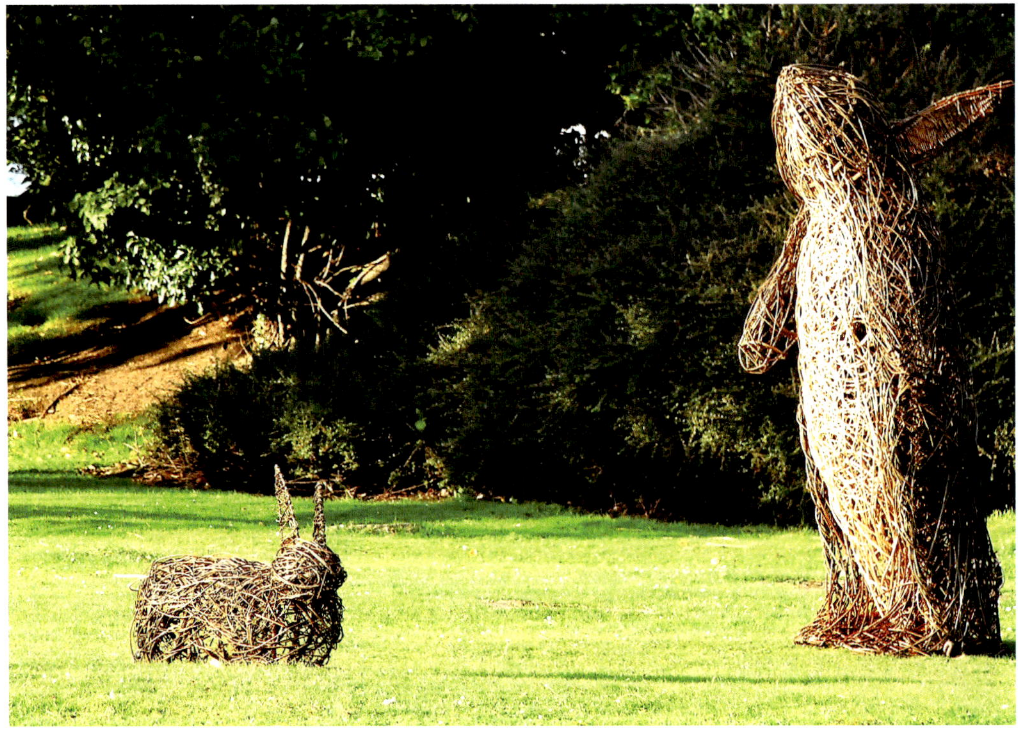

Wicker rabbits on Wall's Roundabout. (Roger Smith)

In 2008 the bunnies even got a website dedicated to them from the family of local resident Gordon Tozer and his wife Janet, as well as their own Twitter and Facebook pages. There were reports of poachers being seen trying to catch the rabbits with nets and there were also fears that someone might even be poisoning the bunnies after several dead bodies were spotted by passing drivers.

In 2009, the City Council added three wicker rabbit sculptures – although they were also known to disappear from time to time and once had to be retrieved from the bedroom of some students living nearby who kidnapped them, presumably after a few drinks!

By 2012, the numbers had dropped from a few dozen to just one or two. In 2022 it was reported that just a single bunny remained and, at the time of writing, none have been seen for quite a while.

Gloucester Characters

Historic
Aethelflaed

Aethelflaed, Lady of the Mercians, was the daughter of King Alfred the Great and ruled Mercia from 911 until her death in 918. She founded St Oswald's Priory in Gloucester. In 2018, a re-enactment of her funeral took place in the city to mark the 1100th anniversary of her death. She is best known for fighting off the Vikings and uniting kingdoms to create England as we know it today. She is also responsible for much of the city centre's street pattern. Her story inspired the Netflix series *The Last Kingdom* and the character Eowyn in Tolkien's *Lord of the Rings*.

She is believed to be buried at St Oswald's Priory and a very ornate gravestone, believed to have come from her grave, was found at St Oswald's and is on display at the Museum of Gloucester. Her body has never been found and could be under a nearby house or even under the road! If it was to be found, it could trigger a media frenzy similar to that experienced in Leicester when Richard III was found in 2012.

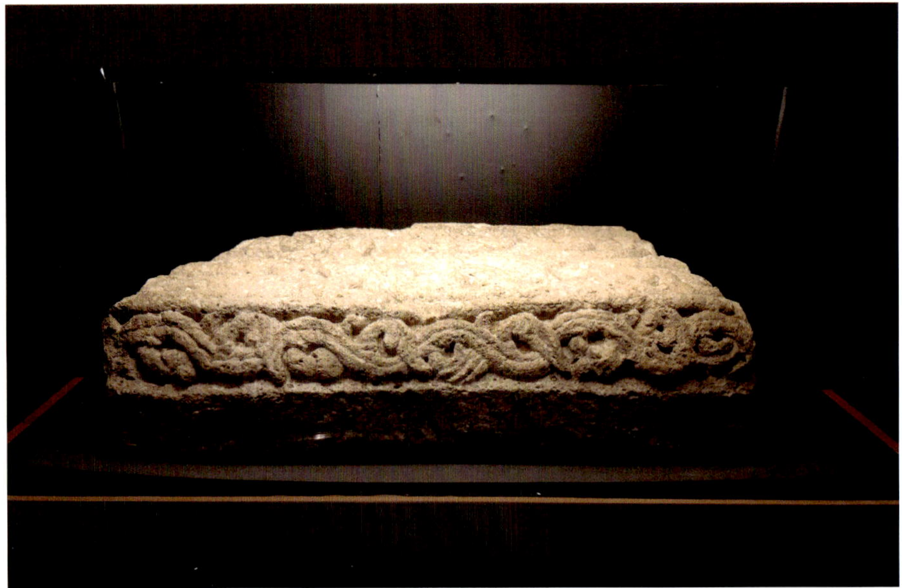

What is believed to be Queen Aethelflaed's gravestone in the Museum of Gloucester. (Reproduced with the kind permission of the Museum of Gloucester)

Jemmy Wood

James 'Jemmy' Wood was reputedly the wealthiest commoner in Victorian England. The source of Jemmy's fortune was owning the Gloucester Old Bank on Westgate Street – on the site of what is now McDonald's. He was notorious for his miserly habits and loathed so much by the local community that they threw stones at his coffin during his funeral procession. It was this unenviable reputation that brought him to the attention of one Charles Dickens, leading him to be immortalised in several novels and countless film and theatre adaptations. He is buried in St Mary de Crypt on Southgate Street.

William E. Henley

The poet William Ernest Henley was born in Eastgate Street, on the site of what is now the Card Factory shop, and attended The Crypt School. He most famously wrote the poem *Invictus* which was read every day by Nelson Mandela whilst in captivity, but was also quoted at different times by Winston Churchill and Barack Obama. It was the inspiration for the 2009 film of the same name about South

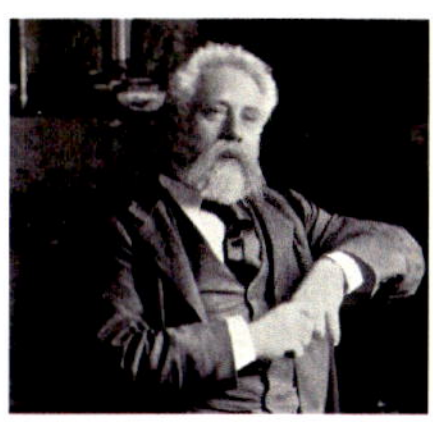

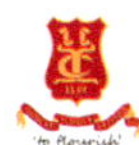

The poem 'Invictus', for which William E. Henley is most famous.

Africa winning the Rugby World Cup in 1995 and for Prince Harry's Invictus Games for injured service personnel.

Henley lost one of his legs after suffering from tuberculosis. He was friends with Robert Louis Stevenson and was the inspiration for the character Long John Silver in his book *Treasure Island*.

Modern Day
Alan Myatt

When something quirky is taking place in the city, Gloucester's Town Crier Alan Myatt is usually at the centre of it. The city's biggest character has held the role for over thirty-five years and is a key figure in most big occasions taking place in Gloucester. He organises the Mock Mayor of Barton inauguration and parade and the Gloucester Day celebrations, which includes a huge parade through the city centre made up of everyone from the mayor to voluntary groups and veterans.

In 2006 he hit the headlines when appearing in pantomime at the New Olympus Theatre as the genie in Aladdin. It was reported that he quit because he was too fat to burst through the stage's trapdoor – the 23-stone town crier's 56-inch waistline kept getting wedged in the hole and bosses feared it was a health and safety risk. Alan, who was forty-nine at the time, said: 'I'm just too big to be the genie anymore. The time has come to hang up my lamp. I'm not as agile as I used to be.' The trapdoor at Gloucester's New Olympus Theatre had been widened two years previously to accommodate Alan's expanding figure.

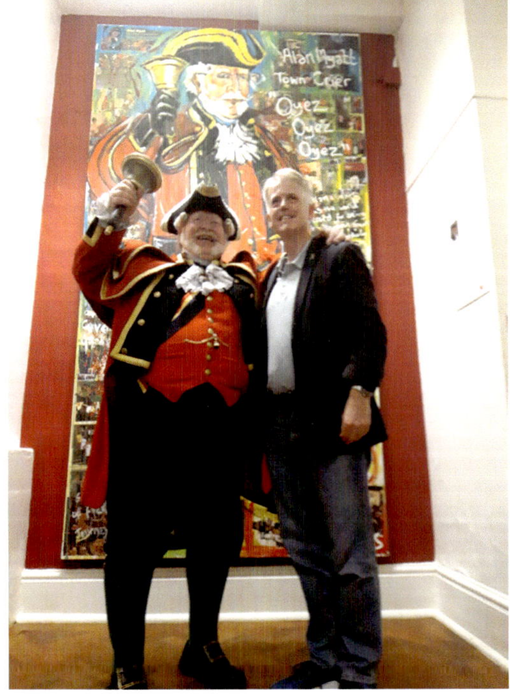

Gloucester's Town Crier Alan Myatt with author Paul James.

The *Daily Mirror* used a particularly cruel headline of 'Genie of the Lump'. The story even made it onto BBC's *Have I Got News For You?* with an image of Alan and a bemused theatre set-builder Gordon Higgs appearing in the Odd One Out round.

Don Weston

Many people feel that they have suffered at the hands of Gloucester's growing seagull population over the years. But few can have suffered to the same extent as the late Don Weston, former operator of Sir Thomas Rich's car park on the corner of Hampden Way and Wellington Street in the city centre.

'Seagull Don', as he became known, became famous across the world after enduring regular attacks every summer from a seagull dubbed the 'Wellington Bomber'. The pesky bird dive-bombed him for six long summers starting in the mid-1990s. Film and pictures of Don running for cover across his Wellington Street car park with the angry gull attacking him were published and broadcast worldwide .

He appeared on German TV and was even invited to set the balls for the Italian national lottery! He also became popular in Japan.

After several years of being regularly targeted by his nemesis gull, Don published a children's book, *The Adventures of Don and Swoop*, about his

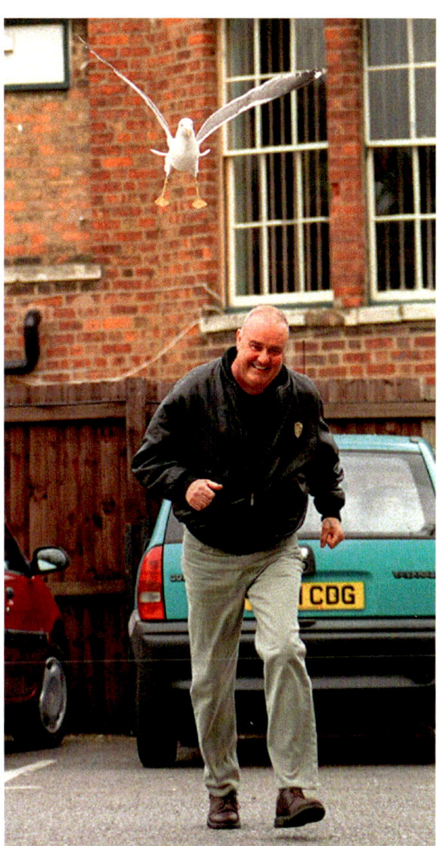

Don Weston being chased by a gull across his car park. (Paul Nicholls)

experiences. He paid to publish 2,000 copies and sold them in aid of the Motor Neurone Disease Association, a charity he regularly supported.

Don lived for many years in Hempsted where he had a painting of the gull attacking him on his wrought-iron gates.

Don wasn't the only Gloucester figure to suffer at the hands of a seagull. Gloucester Mayor Harjit Gill was photographed after being hit by seagull mess in 2007.

Luke Cameron

Luke Cameron, at the time marketing manager for Gloucester shelving company BiGDUG, was dubbed the 'Nicest Man in Britain' in 2014 after completing 365 days of good deeds.

He beat thousands of candidates from across the world to be given the 'Nicest Job in Britain'. His challenge was to travel the country helping forty-five different charities over fifty-two weeks.

In 2019, he unveiled the 'largest advent calendar in the UK' in Gloucester – with acts of kindness set to appear in each window at the company's headquarters on Bristol Road. A different window display illuminated every day to signify a new act of kindness.

The advent calendar has been repeated in subsequent years. In 2023, two dozen heartwarming designs, penned by local children, were chosen to create the calendar – each revealing the inside story on what Christmas means to them.

Each morning as the big day approached, one window was opened to reveal the latest endearing design and message, while matching Christmas cards were sold through the Gloucester Rugby Foundation to raise cash for local community projects. BiGDUG is, at the time of writing, Gloucester Rugby's major sponsor.

Frank Tunbridge

Nature enthusiast Frank Tunbridge from Podsmead in Gloucester has spent many years recording big cat sightings in Gloucester, the wider county and beyond, including in Barnwood and Brockworth.

Several of the sightings have stayed with him as they were clear visions with great detail. He accepts that sometimes miss-sightings can be down to too much alcohol or simply getting it wrong, but still firmly believes that many of the reports which were forwarded to him over decades are true.

Mel Glass

Cycling instructor Mel Glass rides around Gloucester on his modern penny-farthing in Edwardian clothing, but also has a Victorian outfit, complete with top hat, made during the era on Barton Street in the city.

'Every ride on a penny-farthing is an occasion to get dressed up,' he said. 'Quite often, I'm out there in Edwardian tweeds, plus-fours, bright socks, and a bowler hat because it feels right.'

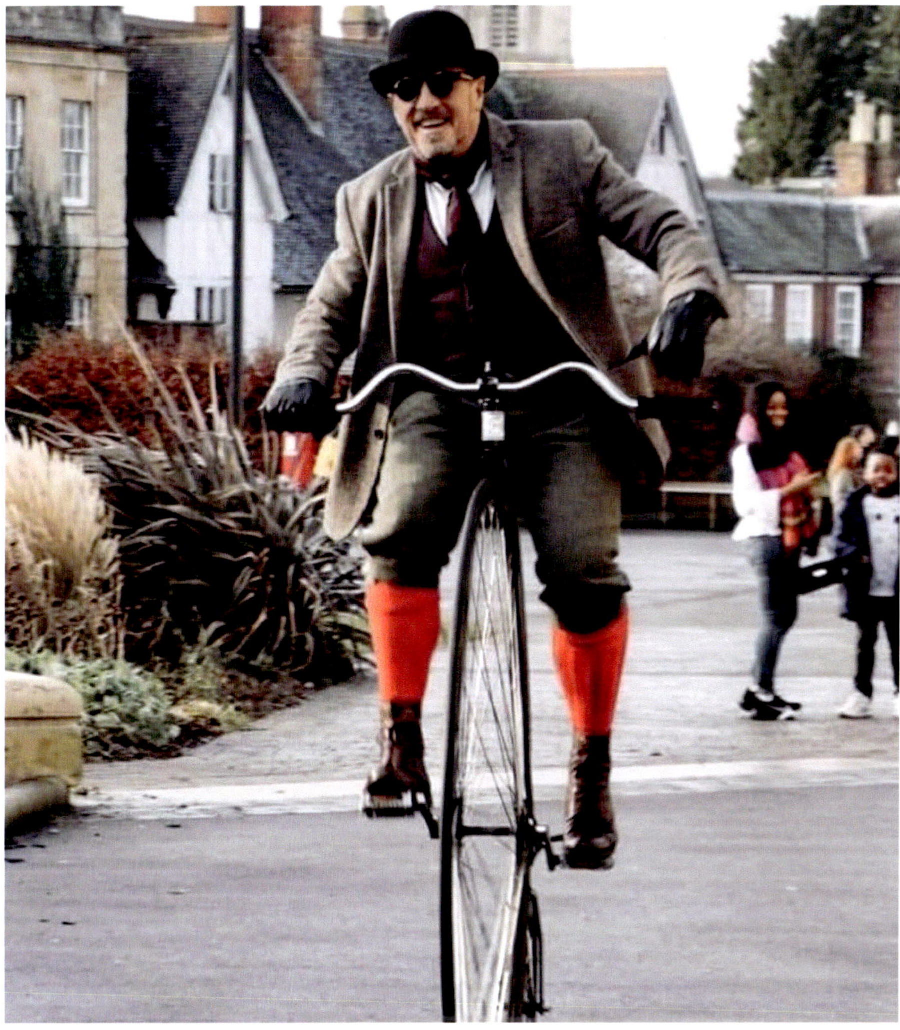

Cycling enthusiast Mel Glass on his penny-farthing.

Mel retired from developing new businesses to become a cycling instructor initially in London and now in Gloucester. Mel lives in Longlevens.

Every April Mel joins other penny-farthing riders on the annual pilgrimage to the grave-side of Robert Stevens in East Finchley, North London. Robert was the first person ever to ride a penny-farthing around the world, completing his three-year journey in 1886.

In October 2024, he was part of the world's longest penny-farthing 'stack', with 140 riders from across the world forming a self-supporting line and holding their position for three minutes at an extravaganza in London.

Mel has now set up the Gloucestershire Penny Farthing Riders Club which, at the time of writing, has two members!

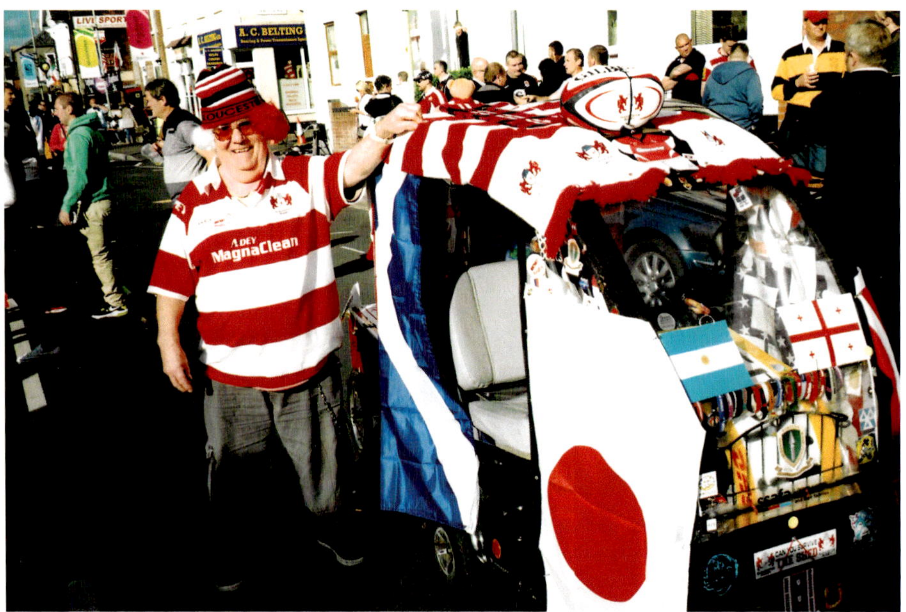

Tony Triffit with his decorated mobility scooter during the Rugby World Cup 2015.

Tony Triffit

Tony, from Podsmead, can often be spotted around the city on his mobility scooter, pulling along a trailer, which is decorated with Gloucester Rugby memorabilia and at Christmas time is adorned with festive lights. He has been known to travel as far as Cheltenham and even Worcester on his scooter.

In 2019, it was reported that he had received a fine for driving the scooter over Llanthony Bridge at Gloucester Docks. The fine was later rescinded after the council admitted the driving ban wasn't intended to apply to mobility scooters.

Eddie Fry

Eddie Fry was known as Gloucester's 'Pocket Hercules'. Just 5 feet tall and slight of build, weighing just 8 stone, he was as strong as an ox. One feat was to hold a three hundredweight anvil on his chest and invite volunteers from the audience to hit it with 14-lb sledge hammers. For an encore, Eddie would lie on a bed of nails with a plank across his chest and another across his stomach. Six men then stood on the chest plank while six others jumped up and down on the stomach plank.

Eddie gave his first public show as a strongman in the skittle alley at the India House pub in 1937. A report with pictures was published in *The Citizen* newspaper and it wasn't long before he was in demand to give shows at clubs, pubs, mission halls and the city hospital. He gave his first theatre show at the Theatre Deluxe in Northgate Street in Gloucester. Other venues for his strongman shows included the County Arms in Millbrook Street and Tredworth Rugby Club. His bed of nails, anvil and springs are now in the Museum of Gloucester's collection.

Unusual Collections and Exhibits

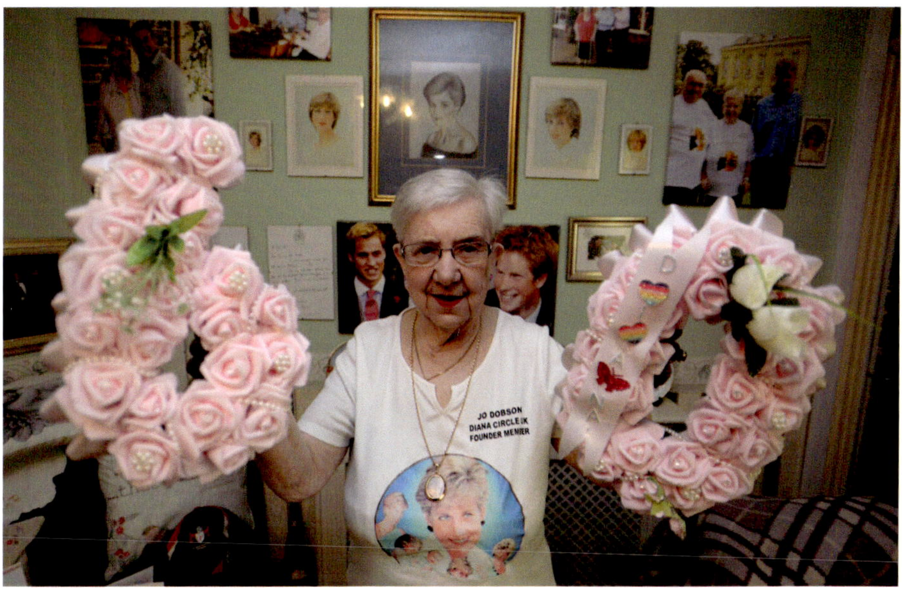

Jo Dobson at home with her collection of Princess Diana memorabilia. (Paul Nicholls)

The Shrine to Princess Diana

Mrs Jo Dobson from Gloucester, along with her late husband Ken, were founders of the Princess Diana Circle, which is dedicated to keeping the memory of the late Princess of Wales alive. Over the years, the Dobsons collected literally hundreds of pieces of Diana memorabilia which filled their home in Hucclecote, which is nothing short of a shrine to her. Mrs Dobson lent part of her collection to the Gloucester Life Museum (now The Folk of Gloucester) for a special exhibition to mark the twentieth anniversary of Diana's death in August 2017.

The Table Football Collection

On a business park at Churcham, just outside Gloucester, is one of the biggest table football collections anywhere in the world. It was put together by Keith Littler, a former football commentator who now runs a TV production company. It is based at his studios and was the focal point of the making of 'Football: The Table-Top Years' – a two-hour documentary following the post-war history of table football in the UK, which is available on DVD.

Keith Littler also produces and presents the 'Table Football Monthly' podcast on YouTube which is described as 'a monthly magazine about all things table football, featuring product tests, reviews, demonstrations and a prize-winning challenge'. At the time of writing it has over 5,000 subscribers.

George Ridgeon

Disabled former fireman George Ridgeon had a penchant for collecting strange artefacts and was a keen bidder at auctions. The items that he acquired that way included Sir Winston Churchill's false teeth, a dress that belonged to Shirley Bassey, Tommy Cooper's stage prop chicken and various items that had been owned by Doris Day, whom he referred to as his 'first girlfriend'.

George stood for election to Parliament in both Gloucester and Cheltenham, at different times, as candidate for the Monster Raving Loony Party.

Museum of Gloucester Collection

The Museum of Gloucester, based in Brunswick Road, has a remarkable collection of objects, totalling around 750,000 items – and still counting!

Amongst the items on display, there are the remains of a Cetiosaurus (a dinosaur found in Gloucestershire), some Megalosaur teeth and the remains of an Ice Age mammal, which is at least 12,000 years old! Other quirky objects include a Roman baby feeder and a medieval ice skate made from animal bone.

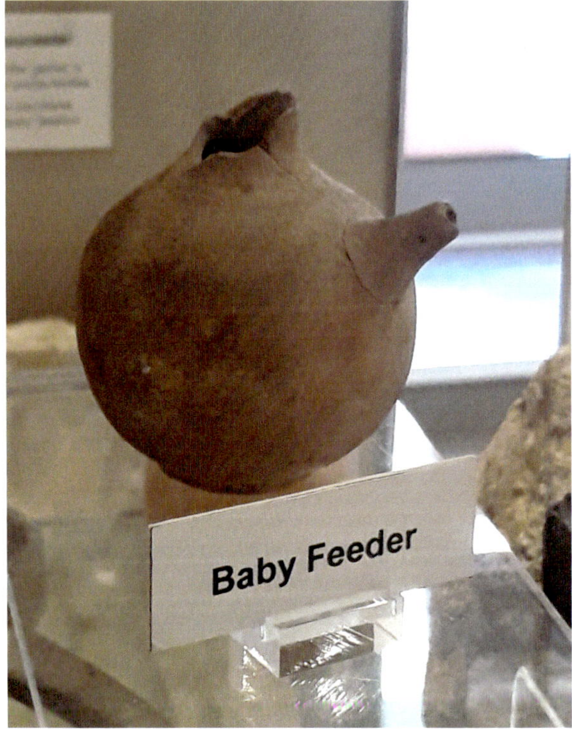

A Roman baby feeder in the Museum of Gloucester. (Reproduced with the kind permission of the Museum of Gloucester)

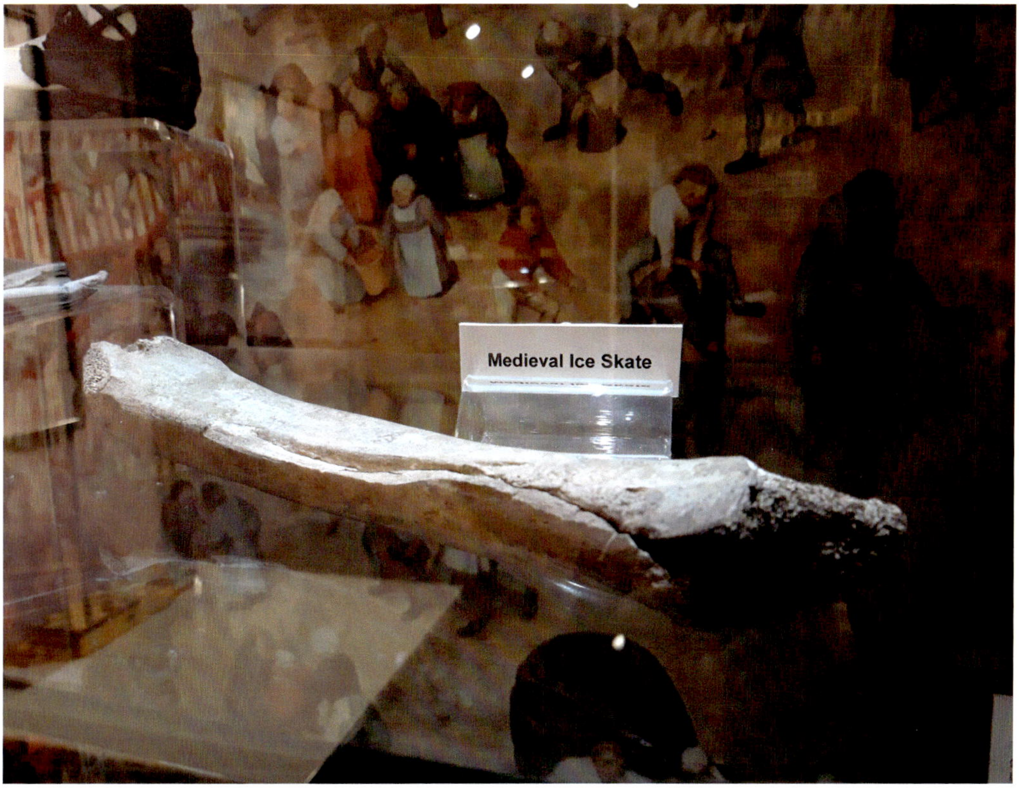

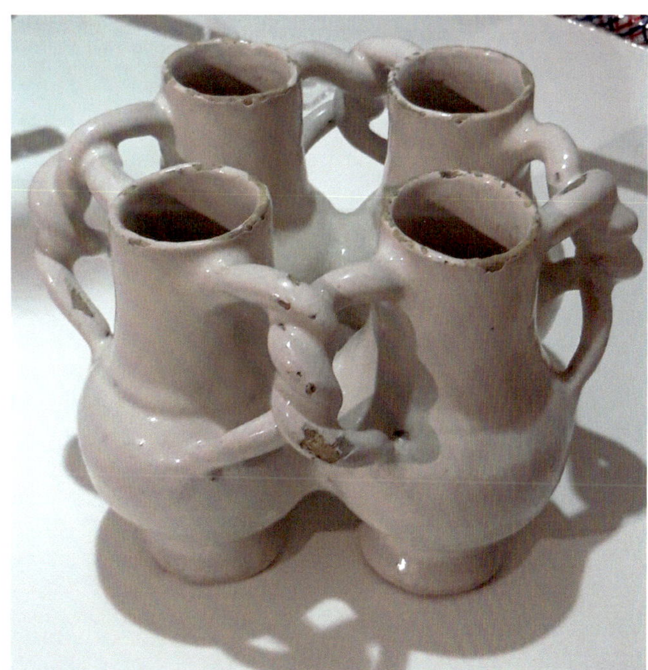

Above: A medieval ice skate in the Museum of Gloucester. (Reproduced with the kind permission of the Museum of Gloucester)

Right: A medieval fuddling cup. (Reproduced with the kind permission of the Museum of Gloucester)

The museum has a 'Fuddling Cup' from the 1600s, which is used in a medieval drinking game. The idea is to fill up each of the four cups and try to drink from it without spilling anything!

Two items from the museum's collection deserve a special mention.

The Birdlip Mirror

In 1879 workmen discovered three skeletons in a quarry between Crickley and Birdlip overlooking the Vale of Gloucester. With the bones were some amazing Iron Age artefacts. The most important object is a handheld mirror of bronze. The front of this was originally highly polished for reflections, but the rear is decorated with flowing patterns worked into the metal. It is one of the finest items of Celtic art to survive in Britain and perhaps the finest example housed outside a national museum. It is one of only sixty found in the world and, based on its appearance, belonged to a wealthy owner.

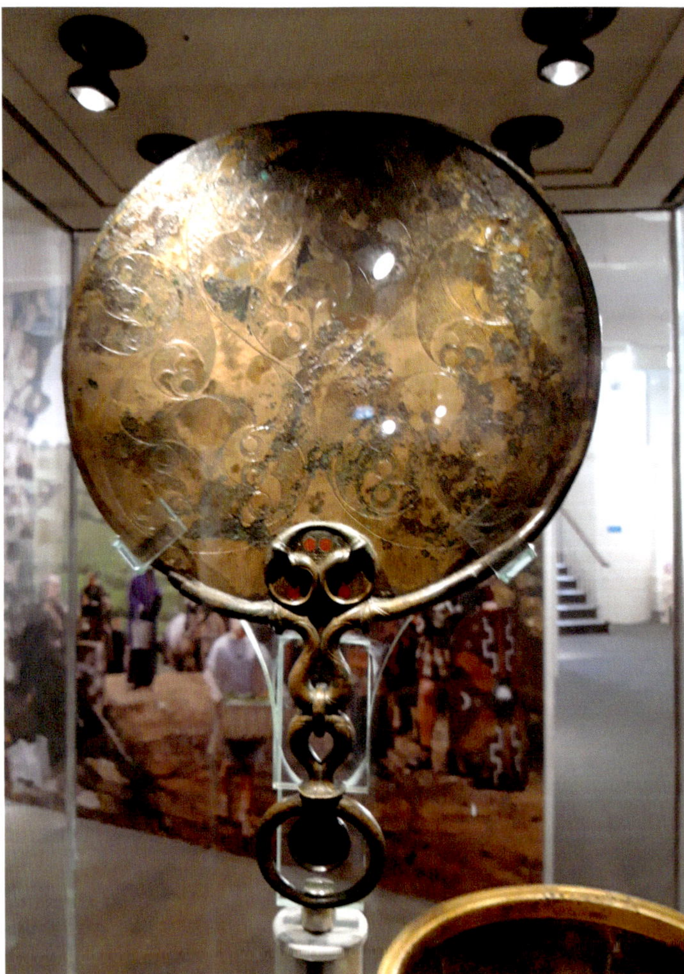

The Birdlip Mirror. (Reproduced with the kind permission of the Museum of Gloucester)

Its true significance is unknown and there are many mysteries surrounding the people it was buried with. The mirror and a reconstructed version of the head of the lady it was buried with are on permanent display at the Museum of Gloucester.

The Gloucester Tables Set

The Gloucester Tables (or Tabula) Set is the earliest surviving board and complete set of counters for the game tabula, which is believed to be the predecessor of backgammon. Dating from the eleventh or early twelfth century, it is an example of Romanesque art. It was discovered in a rubbish pit during archaeological investigations on the site of Gloucester Castle in 1983. The board is Anglo-Saxon whilst the pieces are carved in the Norman style. It is the only complete tabula set ever found. It is now on display in the Museum of Gloucester.

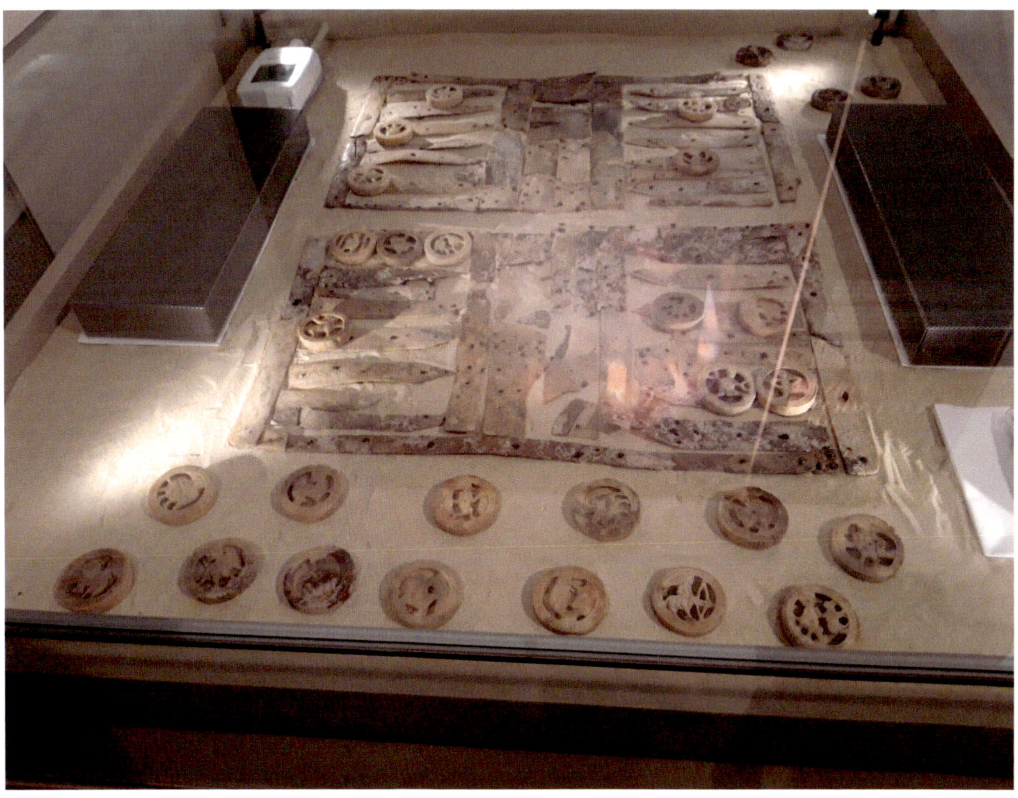

The Gloucester Tabula Set. (Reproduced with the kind permission of the Museum of Gloucester)

Unusual Public Art

Charles II Statue

Tucked away by some former council flats, just off Three Cocks Lane in the city centre, is a Grade II listed statue of King Charles II. The statue was carved in 1662 by Stephen Baldwyn and was originally in the Wheat Market in Southgate Street.

It was removed in the middle of the eighteenth century and its whereabouts remained a mystery until 1945 when it was rediscovered in pieces at Chaxhill, to the west of Gloucester. It was placed in its current location in the 1960s and is in a fairly poor condition; it is very faded and is missing its right arm.

Some say that its unusual location is the city expressing its opinion on the former monarch, who tore down Gloucester's walls in 1662 after the city famously sided with the Parliamentarians during the English Civil War.

In 2022, local councillor Jeremy Hilton was reported as saying the statue should be 'chucked in the canal' in revenge for the King's actions.

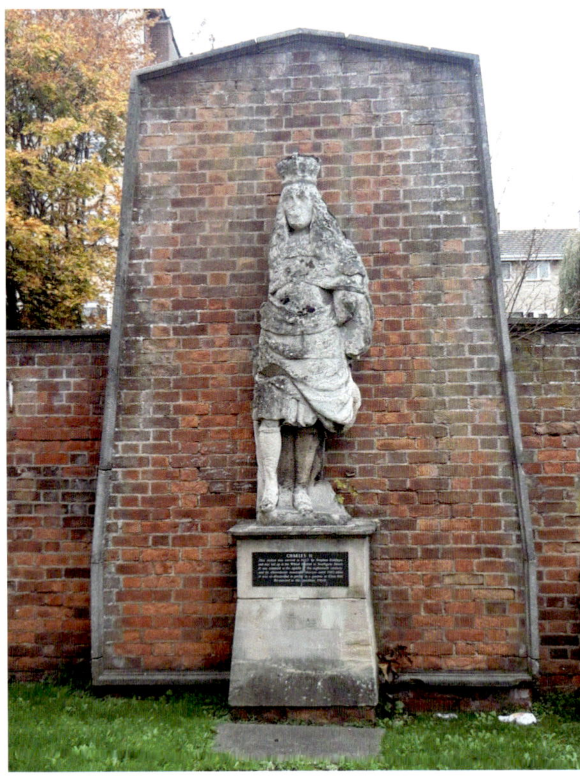

A statue of King Charles II hidden away near the bottom of Westgate Street.

Queen Anne Statue, Gloucester Park

Tucked away on the edge of Gloucester Park, next to The Spa cricket ground, is a statue of Queen Anne by John Ricketts the Elder, who became a Freeman of the City of Gloucester in 1711 in return for making this statue.

It was erected in 1712 near the top of Southgate Street, and moved several times before arriving in Gloucester Park in 1865. It is now in very weathered condition. In the early 2000s, vandals knocked the head off the statue. At the time, as Leader of the City Council, I had to be interviewed for television holding the decapitated head under my arm, in one of those 'Alas, Poor Yorick' moments!

Mural at Former Sainsbury's

This mural, by Henry and Joyce Collins, was installed on the Hare Lane side of the Sainsbury's supermarket when it opened in 1970 in Northgate Street. The Collins' were innovative in their use of colour on concrete murals. This mural features elements of Gloucester's history, including the Roman and Saxon periods. Sainsbury's closed in 2021 and planning consent was granted for fifty-five flats on the site in 2024. One of the conditions of the planning consent was that the mural had to be kept, with a proposal to relocate it to the Northgate Street entrance lobby.

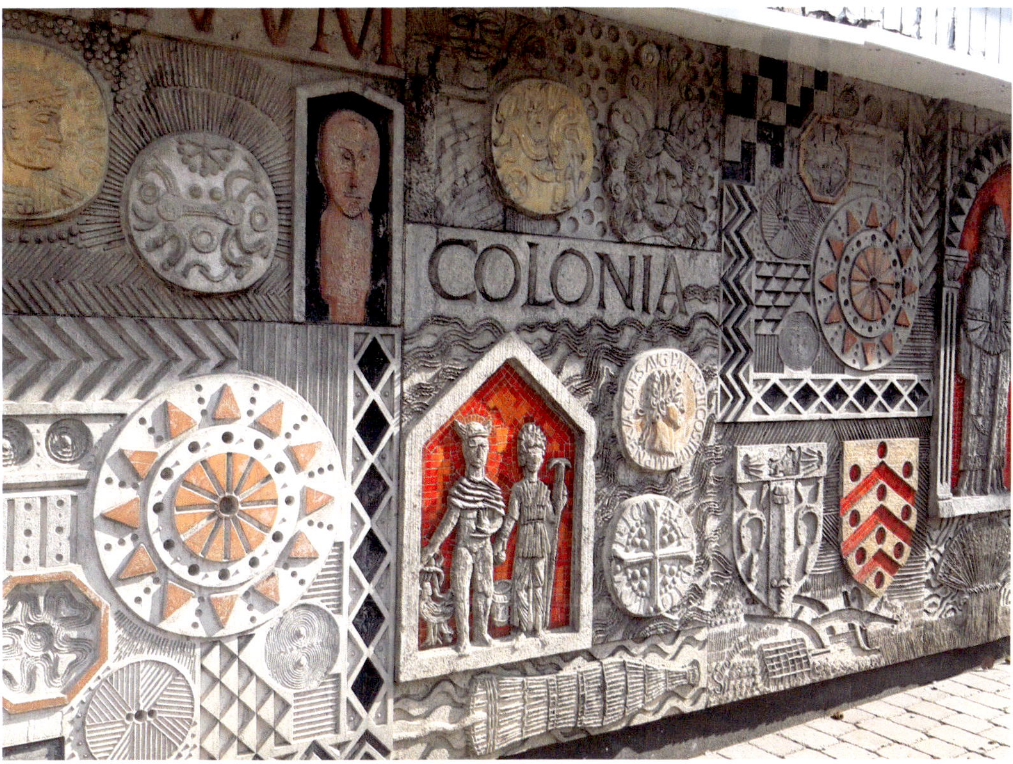

A mural at the rear of the former Sainsbury's store in Hare Lane.

Mural at Former BHS

The same artists produced another concrete and ceramic mural which was for many years on the outside wall of the former British Home Stores shop in Eastgate Street. It depicted the goods on sale in the shop at the time, ranging from electrical goods to toys, clothes, and food. It was removed when Primark took over the former BHS unit in 2021 and was put in storage until another suitable site could be found.

Roman Mural on the Side of Boots the Chemist, Facing Brunswick Road

A large monochrome sculpture depicting scenes from the Roman occupation of Britain, featuring battle scenes, horseback riders, walls, and forts, can be found on the side of the Boots the Chemist store in Eastgate Street, on the wall facing Brunswick Road. It is adjacent to the site of the city's East Gate, which explains why it is sited here.

Pin Bollards

In the eighteenth century, the city's biggest industry was pin-making. It was said that it employed 1,200 men, women, and children. Some of the city's most prominent buildings have been used for pin-making, including the Folk Museum in Westgate Street and the Irish Club in Horton Road. The unusual bollards in the city centre Gate Streets are said to represent Gloucester's pin-making history.

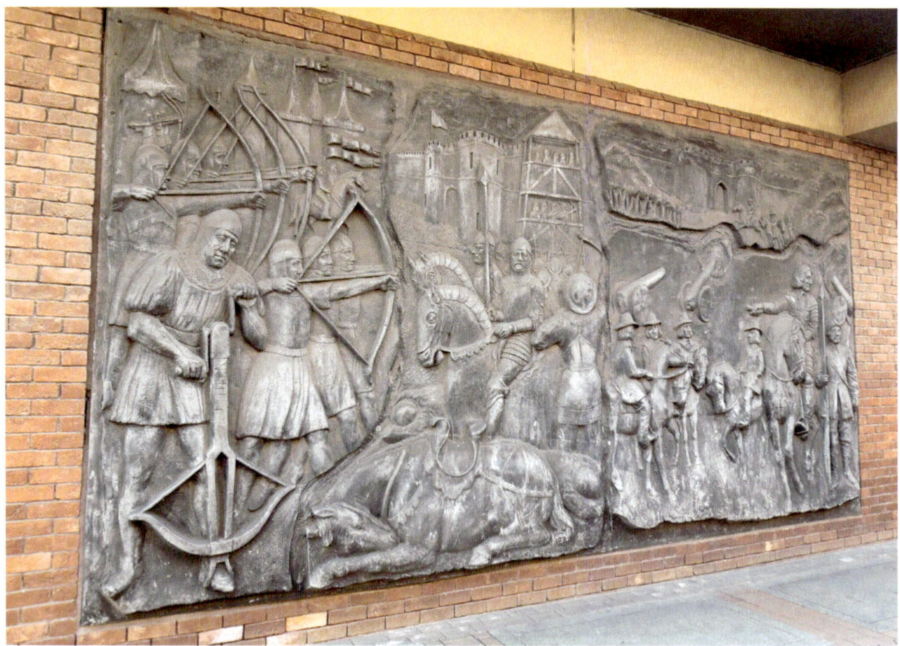

A Roman-themed mural on the side of Boots the Chemist, facing Brunswick Road.

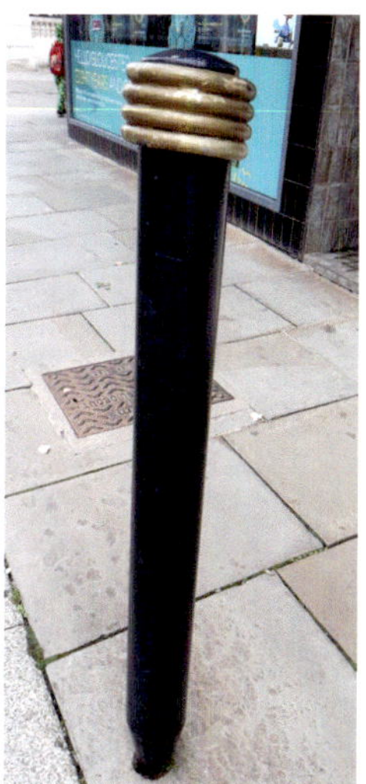

One of the bollards in the city centre gate streets which honours Gloucester's pin-making industry.

The Severn Bore Stone Bench

On The Cross there is a stone bench which is based on the wave of the Severn Bore, which is fitting as the bore passes through Stonebench, near Elmore, 3 miles to the south of Gloucester. The bench has various trades and industries associated with Gloucester featured on the base.

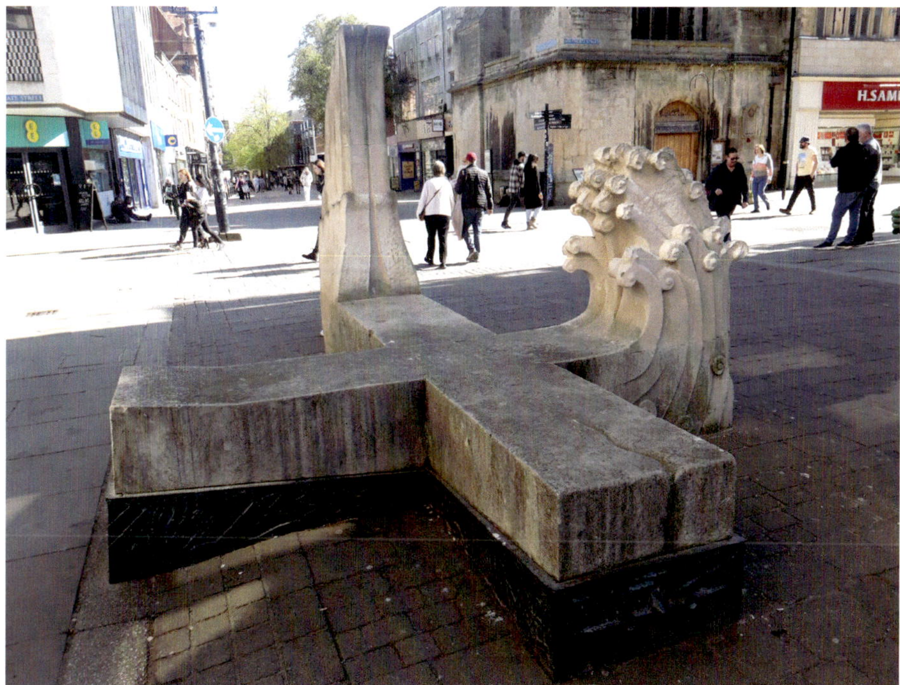

The bench on The Cross which represents the Severn Bore.

The 'Spirit of Aviation' Statue

This statue, by artist Simon Stringer, is sited in Northgate Street by the former Debenhams building. It proved controversial when it was installed in the late 1990s as former workers at the Gloster Aircraft Company, to whom it was supposed to be paying tribute, felt it wasn't an accurate or respectful portrayal of them. The controversy died down and these days it is barely noticed, other than when a seagull or traffic cone ends up on its head!

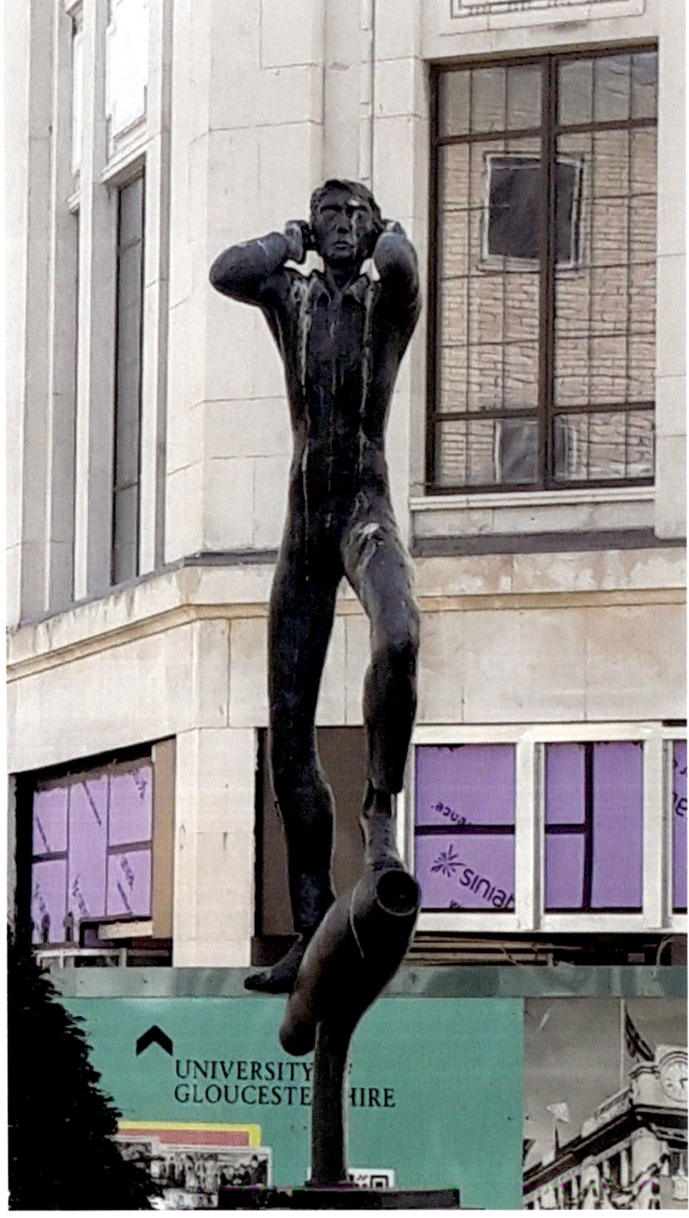

The Spirit of Aviation statue in Northgate Street.

The Emperor Nerva Statue

The most recent statue to go up in the city was Emperor Nerva, who founded Glevum as a Roman colonia. This project was organised by the Civic Trust and the £80,000 cost paid for by public subscription, including a donation from Princess Anne and a £5,000 contribution from the City Council. The horseback sculpture was cast by Anthony Stones.

I was privileged to be there in my capacity as Sheriff of Gloucester, with Pam Tracey as Mayor, when the statue was lowered into place in October 2002. The

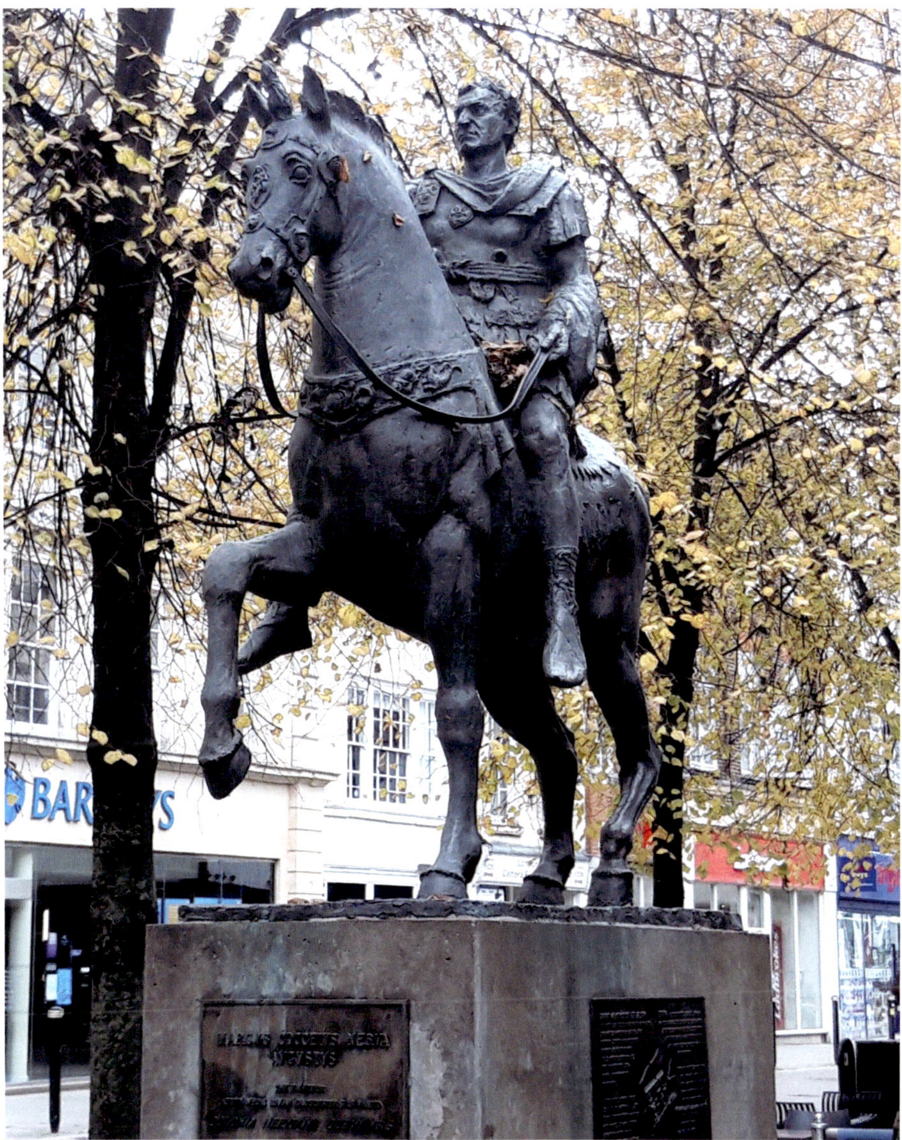

The Emperor Nerva statue in Southgate Street.

statue is located as close as possible to the site of an earlier statue of Nerva, of which bronze remains were found by archaeologist Henry Hurst when the Bell Hotel was demolished in 1969.

The Candle

In the Docks, there is a 23-metre-tall piece of art called 'The Candle' by Wolfgang Buttress, which is a tribute to Ivor Gurney, with his words engraved on the base. Locally it is known as 'The Rusty Needle' or 'The Kebab'.

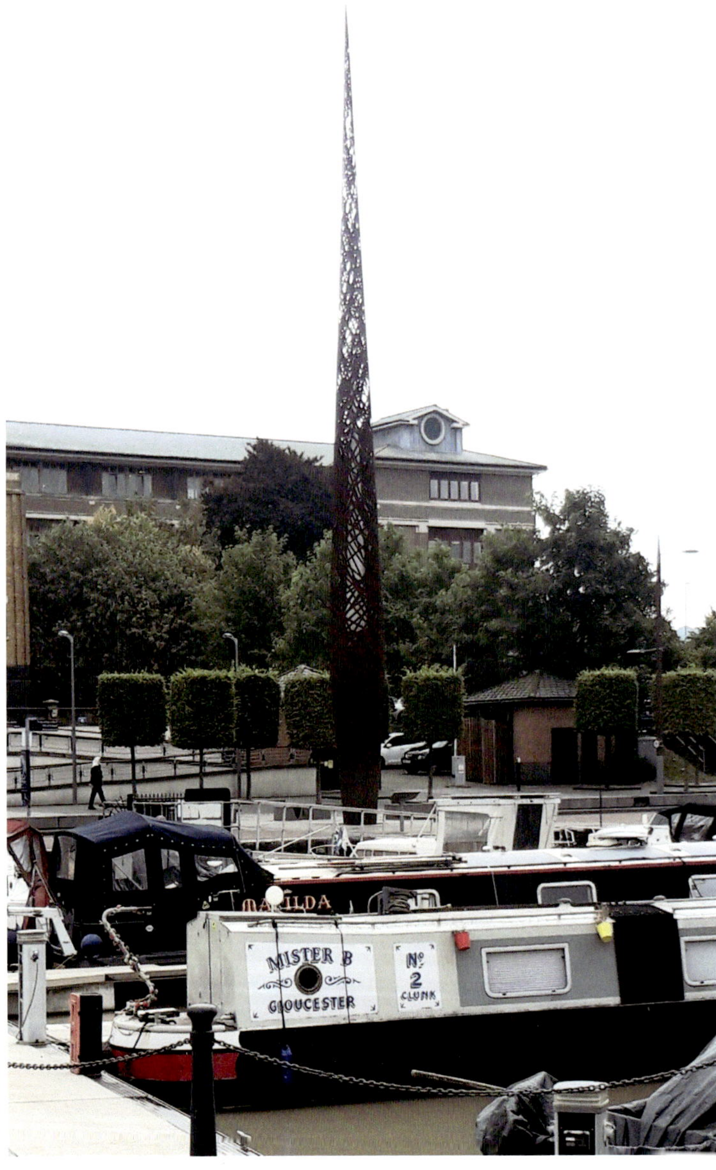

The Candle sculpture in the Docks.

St Kyneburgh's Tower/The CD Rack

Nearby, in Kimbrose Square, there is another piece – 'St Kyneburgh's Tower' by Tom Price. It represents the story of what Price described as 'one of the city's little-known but most captivating legends' of a Saxon Princess who wished to devote herself to God and remain a virgin. To avoid an arranged marriage, she fled to Gloucester and worked as a maid for a baker. The baker's wife, jealous of the young woman, killed her and threw her body into a well near the city's South Gate. Her body was recovered and buried nearby. Miracles began to be

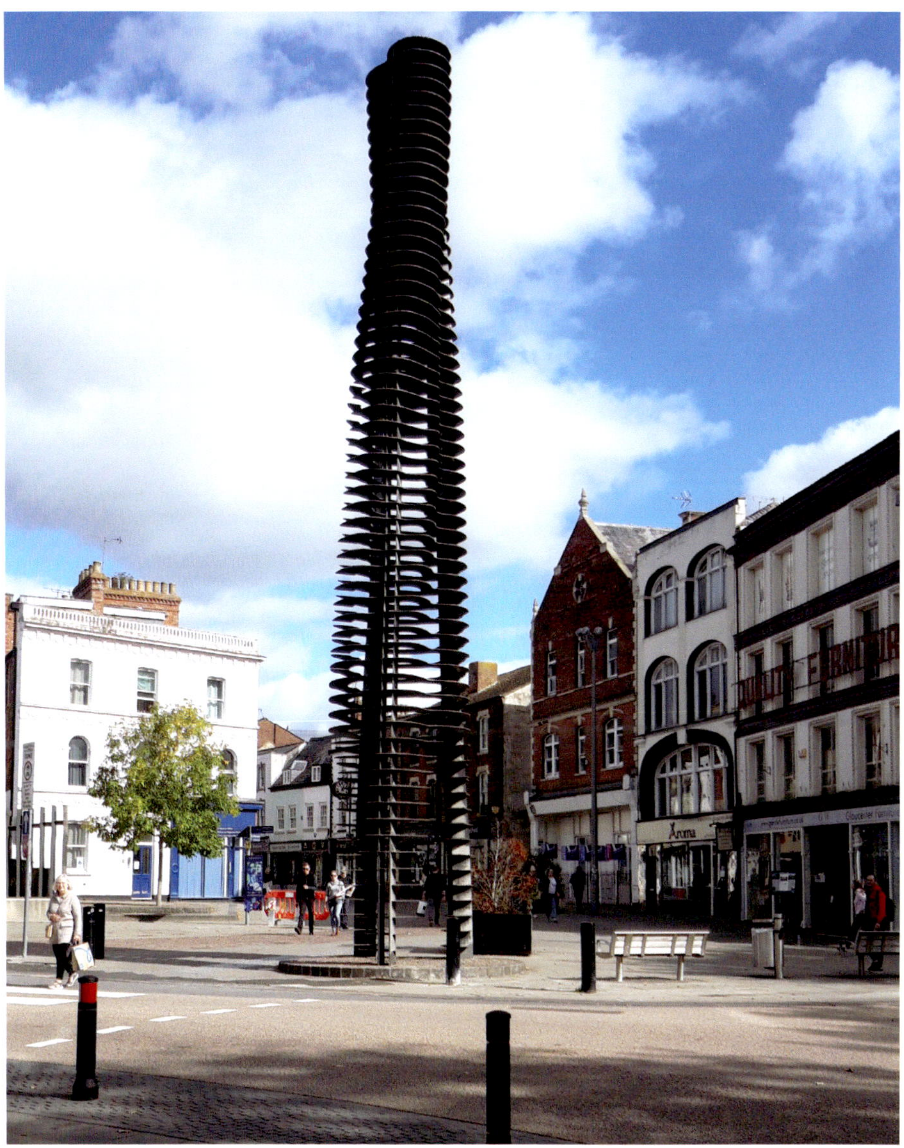

St Kyneburgh's Tower, known locally as 'The CD Rack'.

reported at her graveside, and when the relics were moved, the miracles followed them. The well became known as St Kyneburgh's Fountain, a place of pilgrimage famous for its supposed healing powers. St Kyneburgh's chapel was built there and later converted in the sixteenth century into almshouses by Sir Thomas Bell, who ran a cap factory at the nearby Blackfriars Priory after its dissolution. The structure was designed to replicate the well and if you look up when you're at the bottom of it, that's what it feels like. There is also an accompanying 'art wall' in a similar style, running along the line of the city wall.

There are tacks on the tower to discourage seagulls from perching on it and daredevils and drunks from climbing it. Locally, this structure is known as 'The CD Rack'.

Scrumpty

Scrumpty was Gloucester's mascot for 2015, which was a big year for the city when it hosted four matches for the Rugby World Cup, an Elton John concert at Kingsholm and held the Tall Ships Festival, amongst other things. Scrumpty is a mix of a rugby ball and Humpty Dumpty who, legend has it, was based on a siege engine at Llanthony Secunda Priory during the Civil War.

Sculptures were created by artists, which formed a trail around the city centre and Docks. This included sculptures in the style of a soldier, a monk and the mouse from the Tailor of Gloucester. More than a decade on, several can still be

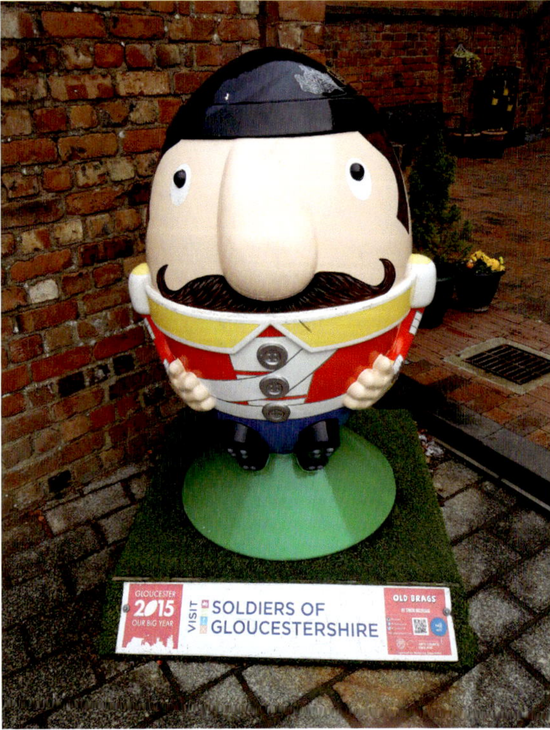

A soldier-themed Scrumpty outside the Soldiers of Gloucestershire Museum.

seen on display, including a soldier at the Soldiers of Gloucestershire Museum and one in a shop window in Southgate Street, as well as numerous smaller versions at locations around the city. Scrumpty also had his own brand of keyrings, lapel badges, fridge magnets, beer and sausages!

The Family Group

The modernist statue the Family Group at the bottom of Westgate Street always divided opinion. The statue was installed in Westgate Street in 1961 at the then recently completed Dukeries development. The 10-foot-tall artwork, cast in concrete, was commissioned by the city council at a cost of £400 from John Whiskerd from Newent, who was a lecturer at Gloucester Art School.

It was removed after the concrete decayed and the statue was decapitated by a visiting football team, who took one of the heads away as a trophy. Rumour has it that the remaining concrete was used as hardcore for a road somewhere in the city.

Cherubs in Three Cocks Lane

This sculpture is on the end of a modern building on the corner of Westgate Street and Three Cocks Lane, which was for a number of years 'The Gateway' – the City Council's customer reception. The sculpture of the cherubs was actually carved

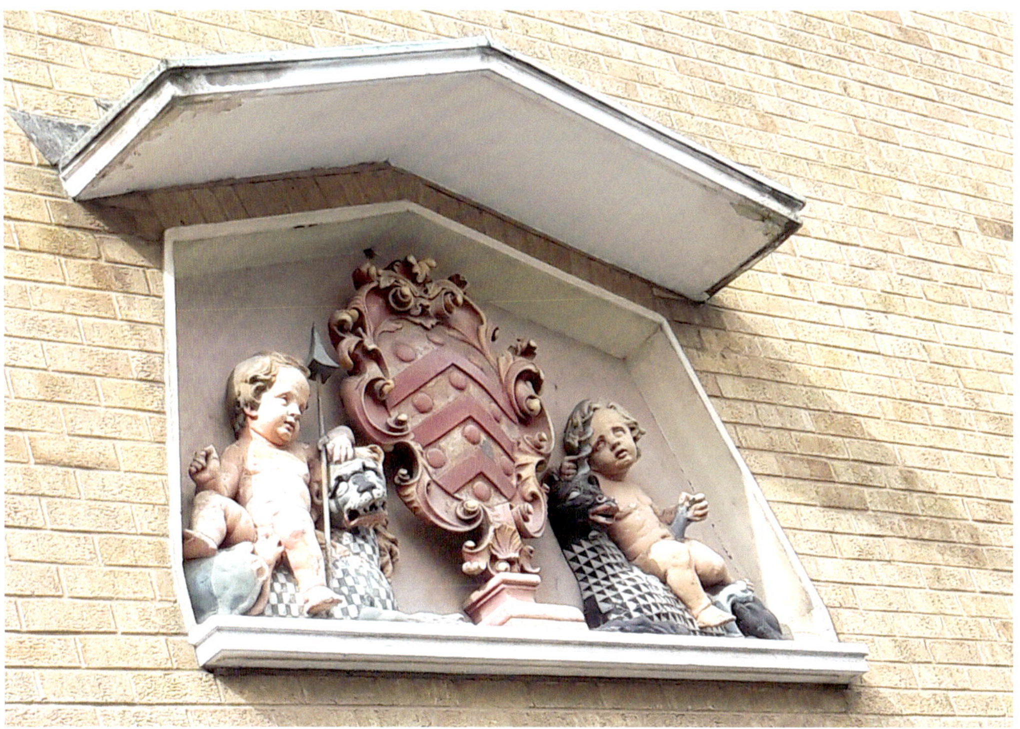

A sculpture of cherubs in Three Cocks Lane.

in the eighteenth century to adorn the pediment of the Booth Hall, a former civic building and later entertainment venue which stood in Westgate Street. The Booth Hall was demolished in 1957, but the sculpture was moved to this building. The City Council agreed to sell the building in 2024 after moving its customer reception to the Eastgate Shopping Centre. Hopefully the new owners will take care of this quirky feature.

Street Art in the City Centre

In recent years, street art has been introduced to the city centre, including artists painting utility boxes with images associated with the city, ranging from a Roman soldier and the England's Glory matchbox logo, to the face of Gloucester-born Hollywood superstar Simon Pegg.

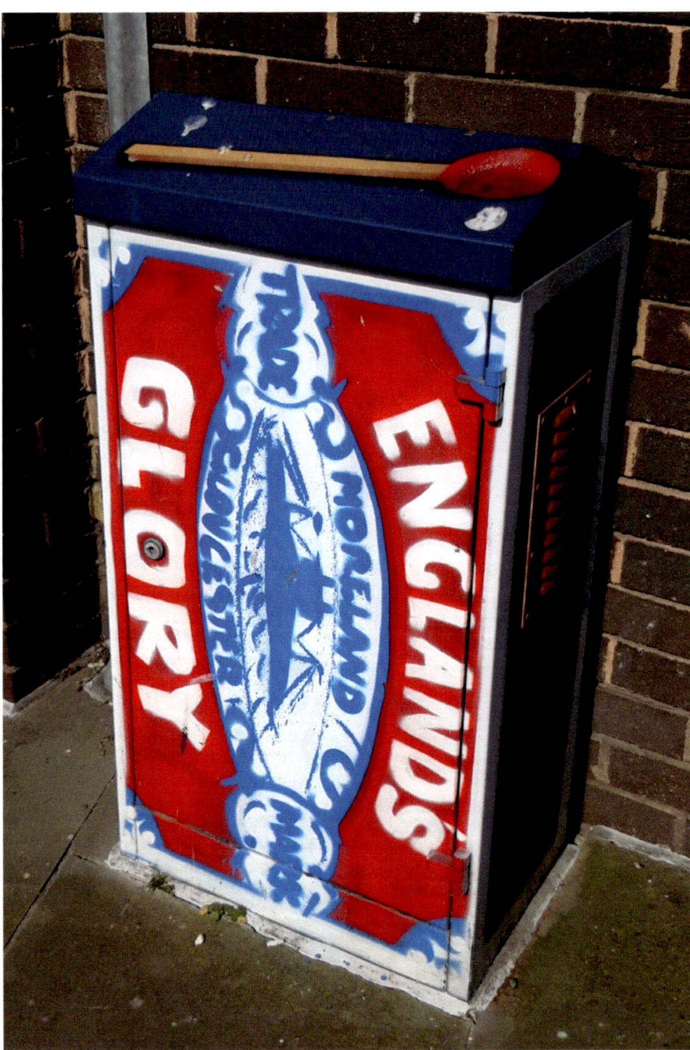

The England's Glory logo painted on a utility box in the city centre.

The Gloucester Window at the Transport Hub

As a nod to Gloucester Cathedral's stained-glass windows, the 'Gloucester Window' was introduced to the Gloucester Transport Hub (or the bus station as most people know it). This features buildings from the city and images representing Gloucester's history. It also shows the word 'Welcome' in a number of different languages. But, as critics pointed out, the 'Welcome' message is seen when you are waiting for a bus – to leave!

The Victorian Drinking Water Fountain

An unusual drinking fountain is located near the North Warehouse in Gloucester Docks. It was installed by the Gloucester City Board of Health at the bequest of merchants on behalf of their workers. Installed in 1863, this water supply was also used to fill ships' water casks.

In 2024, a petition was launched to bring it back into use to keep visitors to the Docks hydrated. The City Council said they would 'respond positively' to the petition, but at the time of writing the fountain still runs dry.

The fountain is featured on the 'Memorial Drinking Fountains' website.

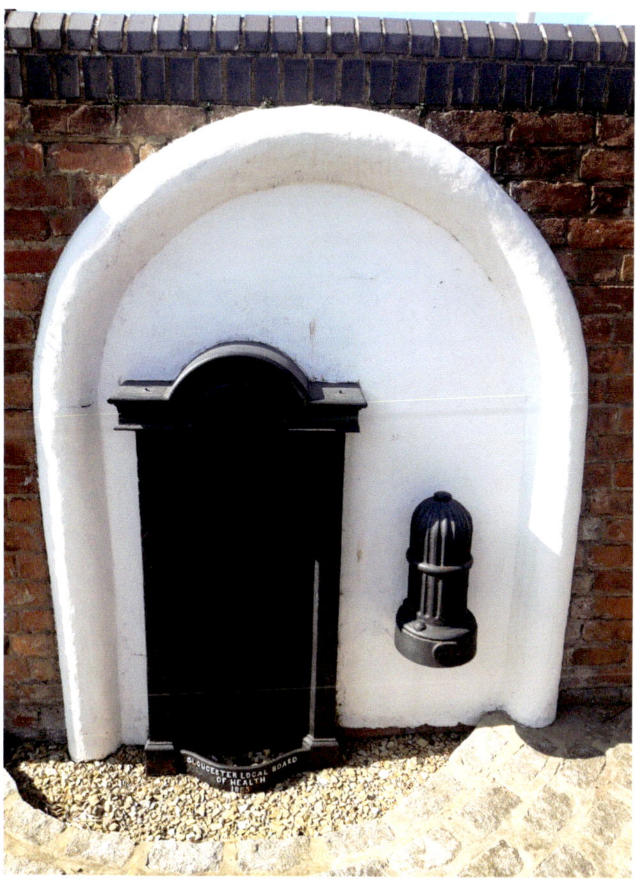

A Victorian drinking
water fountain in
the Docks.

St John's Church Spire

Sitting in St Lucy's Garden, which runs between St John's Lane and Hare Lane, is the former top of the spire of St John's Church in Northgate Street. It was removed for safety reasons when it became unstable and was re-erected here in 1910. The church tower and steeple are medieval and the main body of the church was replaced in 1734.

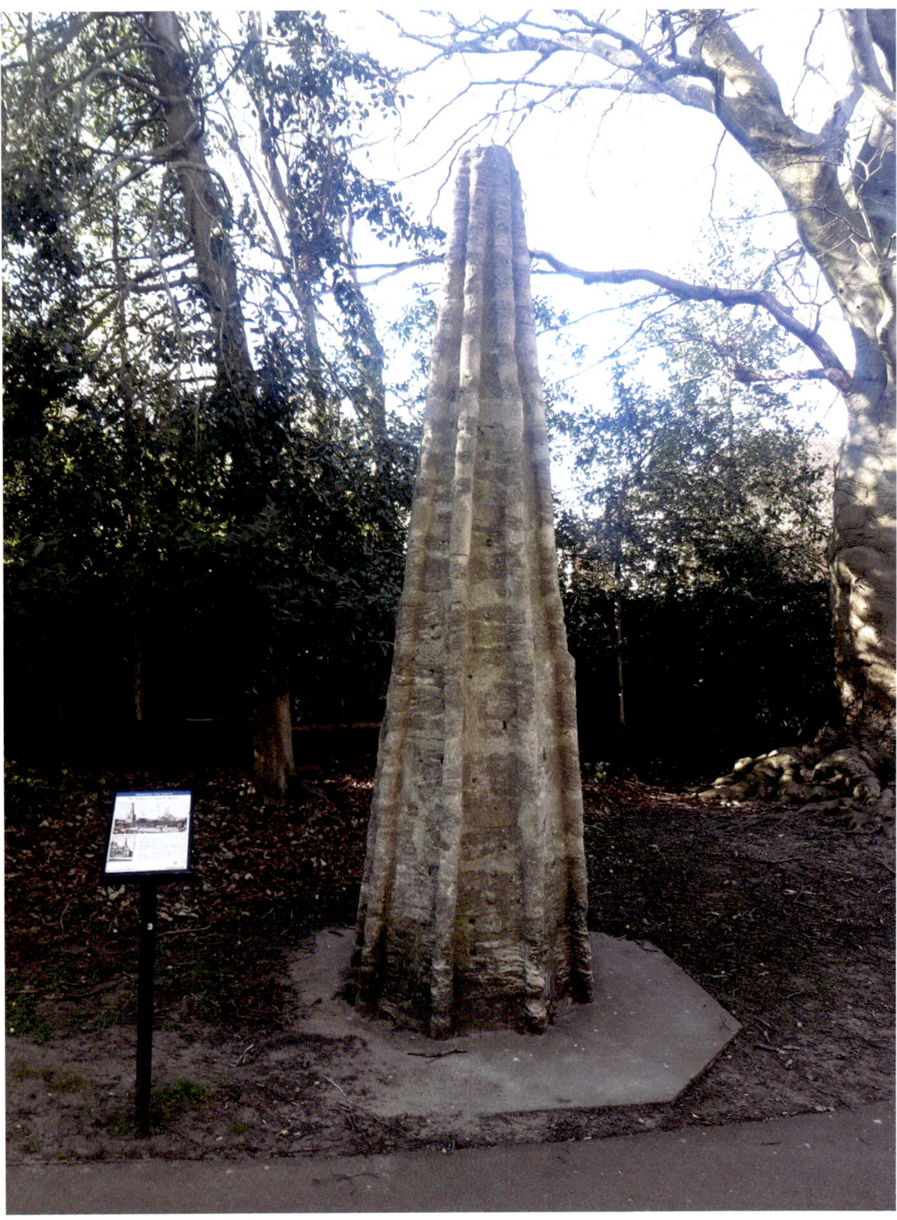

The former spire of St John's Church in St Lucy's Garden in Hare Lane.

Greyfriars Public Art

There is some unusual public art, in the form of benches, provided as part of the Greyfriars development on the former Gloscat campus in the city centre, both on the Brunswick Road frontage (which runs along the line of the city wall) and in the new public square which faces onto the Greyfriars monument.

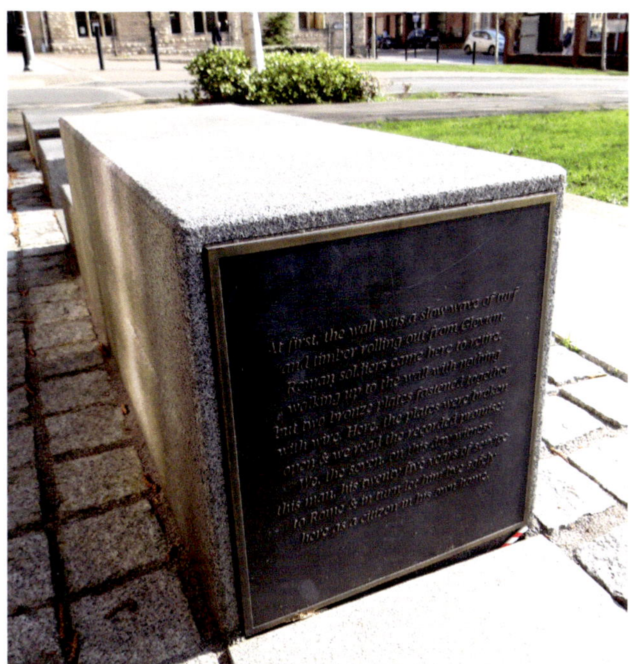

Right and below: Public art benches in the Greyfriars development.

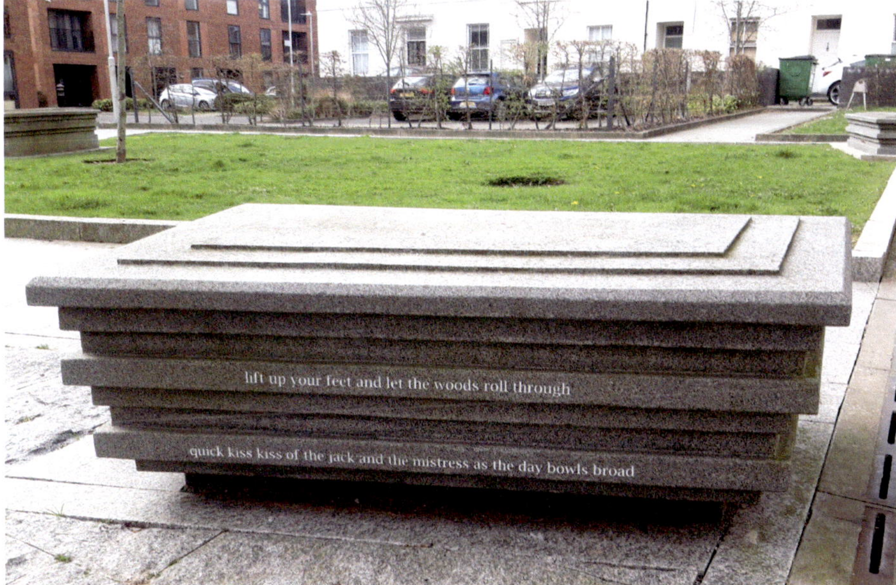

The Brunswick Road benches have inscriptions about historical events, including the Civil War Siege of Gloucester and the Saxon invasion of 577.

Russell Haines

Gloucester's best-known artist is probably Russell Haines. Russell became an artist after suffering a brain stem stroke and having to give up work in 2009. After the stroke led to depression, his GP recommended he should work with charity Artlift which provides free art courses for people with long-term mental and physical health conditions.

Russell paints portraits in his unique style – they are large (typically 6ft tall) and colourful. His 'Tales of a City' exhibition at the GL1 Leisure Centre has been running for a number of years and is made up of portraits of people from Gloucester, ranging from Town Crier Alan Myatt to rugby player Mike Tindall, BBC television reporter Steve Knibbbs and many members of the city's minority ethnic communities.

His work is on display in other locations, ranging from Gloucester Brewery's Warehouse 4 venue, where he is artist in residence, to the Judge's Lodgings in Spa Road, which these days provides Airbnb accommodation for visitors to the city.

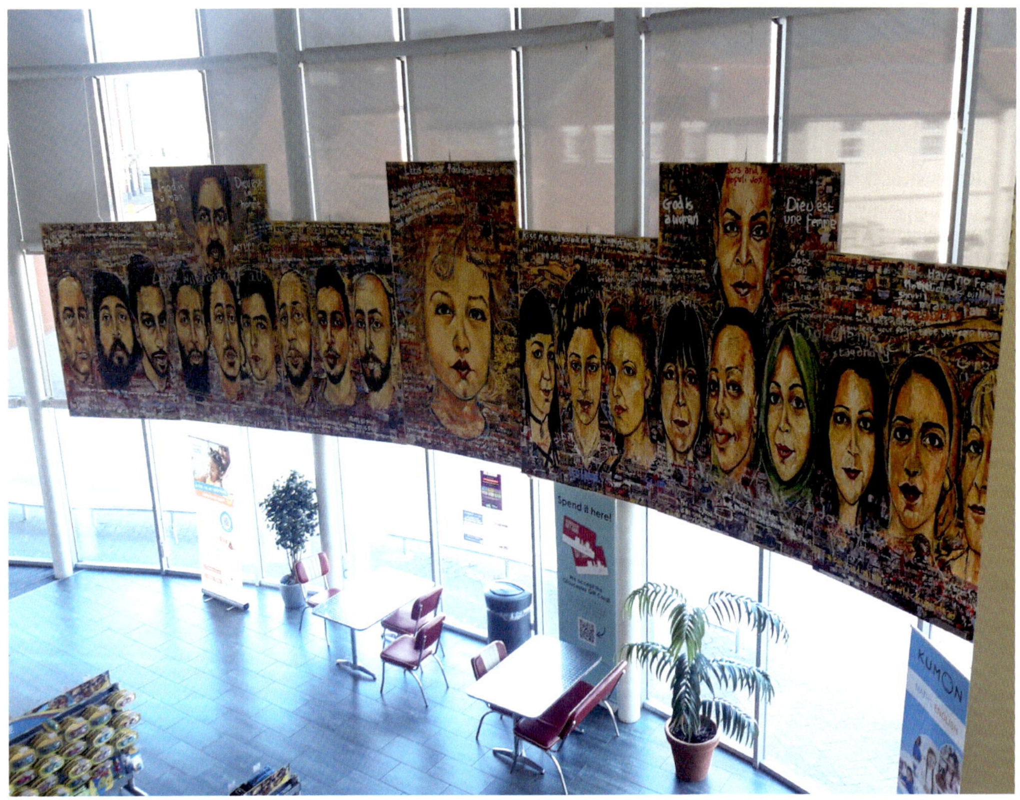

A gallery of Russell Haines' work at the GL1 Leisure Centre.

Cathedral Postbox Toppers

Just inside the cathedral precincts in College Green is a postbox which often has colourful, artistic, themed knitted postbox toppers on it. These are generally made by the owners and staff at the nearby Miju Wools shop in College Street, sometimes with the assistance of their customers.

Over the years, the toppers have celebrated Christmas, Easter and royal events, as well as the visit to the cathedral of the 'Knife Angel' sculpture and a giant bee sculpture. The bee-themed topper caught the eye of HRH The Duchess of Gloucester on a visit to the city for Gloucester Day in September 2022.

The postbox at Hempsted Post Office is another where the local 'Knit and Natter' group have worked their magic to help brighten up the area with their creations.

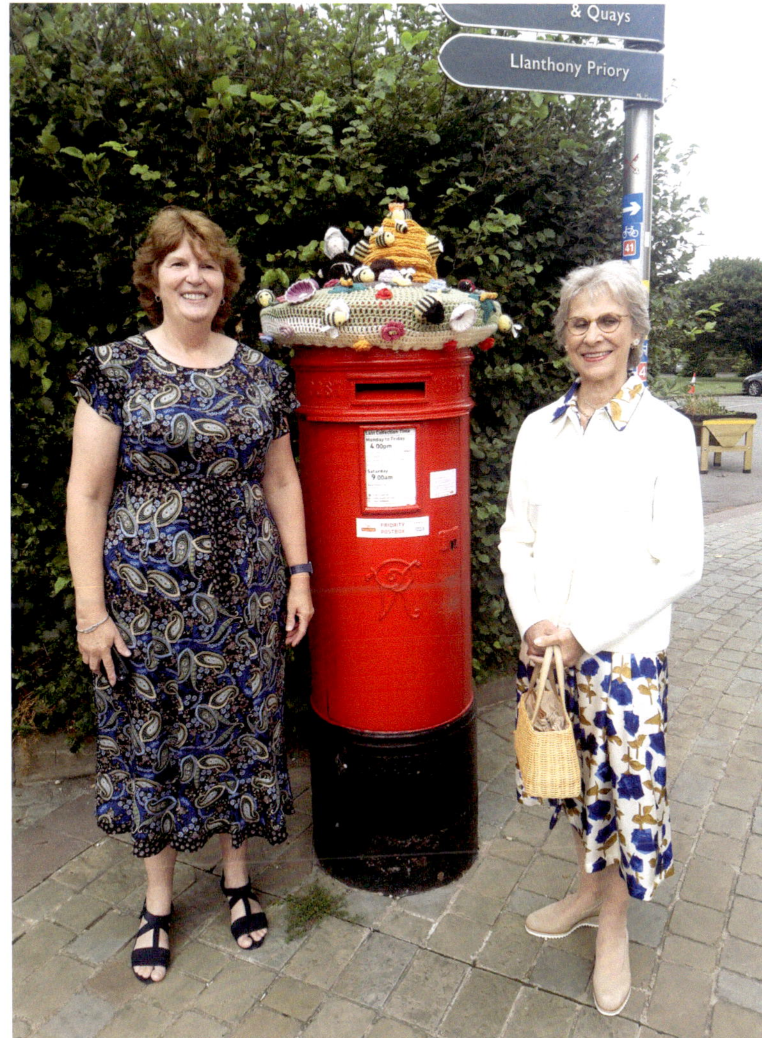

Carol Steele from Gloucester County, Virginia, and HRH The Duchess of Gloucester admiring a postbox topper near Gloucester Cathedral.

Entertainment and Attractions

Ghost Stories

The New Inn is reputed to be one of Gloucester's most haunted buildings. The hotel in Northgate Street dates back to the fourteenth century and was originally built to house pilgrims visiting the shrine of King Edward II at nearby Gloucester Cathedral, and is described as having the finest example of a medieval gallery in Britain.

It is claimed that in 2010 a series of unexplained happenings occurred at The New Inn in the space of a week, including the sound of ghostly footsteps, rattling doors and even a pint of beer mysteriously lifting itself off a table and onto the floor.

Gloucester's 'Ghost Lady' Lyn Cinderey was in the bar at the time of the 'moving pint' incident, taking part in a pub quiz. Lyn said at the time, 'There were a few people in the bar, and four people saw this glass – a full pint – just lift up and fall on the floor. The glass didn't even break.'

'The rest of us looked around and heard the thud. We just couldn't believe it. It was right there in the middle of the quiz. I've been investigating this building for a long time and I've never known it so active,' said Lyn.

Lyn reported some other strange happenings too, saying: 'One of the bar staff has heard footsteps in the cellar when he's been clearing up with nobody else there, and staff have also heard the exit door rattle in the restaurant. Another of the bar staff claims that when he's been clearing up he's felt a cold spot and he's been chilled all over.'

Other incidents include the manager's dog's bowl turning over while he was eating from it and plugs coming out of sockets without being touched.

Lyn appeared on *Great British Ghosts*, a show on UKTV channel Yesterday, presented by Michaela Strachan in 2011, showing Michaela around the New Inn and telling stories of its paranormal activity, including the pint of beer that flew across a table.

SULA Lightship

LV14 SULA has been a landmark on the Gloucester to Sharpness Canal, moored alongside Llanthony Secunda Priory for a number of years. She is a charmingly characterful vessel and is the only lightship in the UK on which you can stay aboard!

Described by the BBC as a 'local celebrity of the Gloucester Docks', the registered lightship was originally called SPURN and was stationed on the Humber Estuary between the 1960s and 1980s, protecting mariners with her rare Fresnel lens which shone for 17 miles.

In the many guises that followed, she served as a historic museum in South Wales, then spent some well-deserved quiet time in Gloucester, as a floating therapy and meditation centre until her new owners, experienced water-dwellers

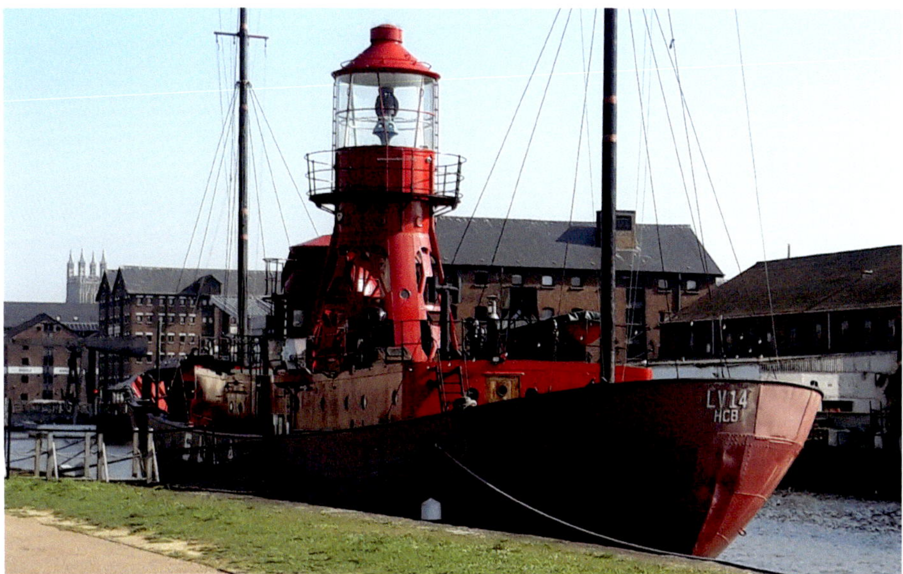

The SULA lightship on the canal near Llanthony Priory.

Colin and Vivienne Brooks, decided to transform the iconic vessel into a stylish holiday retreat.

'Captain' Colin and the Brooks family (including their friendly ship dogs Wilfrid and Whistler) set about painstakingly renovating LV14 SULA, adding flourishes of contemporary style and luxury, whilst ensuring the ship's most precious historic elements were left intact.

Steampunks

The Steampunks of Gloucestershire (the SoG or SoGgies) were formed in 2016 as a local community group for Steampunks and Steampunk curious people in Gloucestershire. Events for the Steampunks have taken place at The Folk of Gloucester and St Mary de Crypt in recent years.

Steampunk is a celebration of the nineteenth-century origins of science fiction. Although the name 'Steampunk' is twentieth century, the style and form of Steampunk goes back to the earliest nineteenth-century authors who created the genre of science fiction.

'Steamers' love dressing up. For some, a lovely Victorian dress or jacket and a fine hat worn at a jaunty angle are enough; for others, well, their own imagination is the limit.

As Steampunk as a movement spread, it encountered the cosplayers, who like to dress up as their favourite characters from comics, TV and film. Trekkies and Jedi are popular costumes but Steampunk has no such limits.

Steampunks do not take themselves seriously. For them, it is all about having fun and escapism. They are proud of being 'a refuge for the outsiders, oddballs, the people that never fitted in with the "right crowd" at school'.

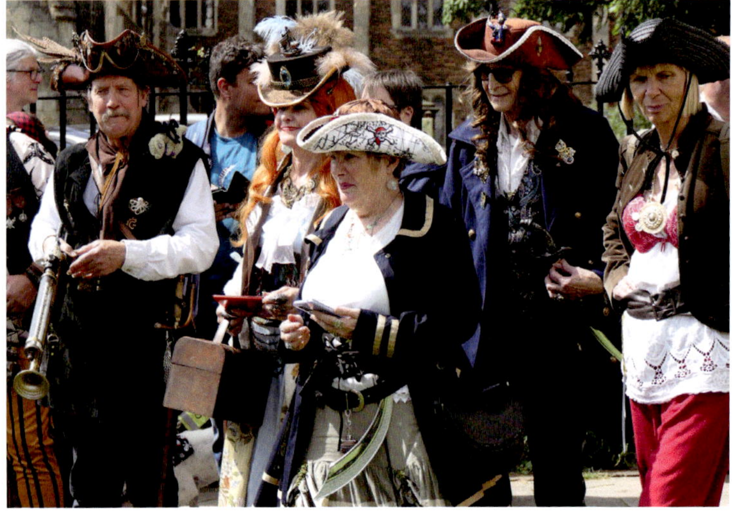

Gloucester's Pirate Walk getting underway. (Martin Adams, Lightspeed Photography)

Gloucester Zombie Walk

The Gloucester Zombie Walk has been taking place for a number of years. It is organised by the team from Café René and sees hundreds of people in some rather scary costumes make their way through the city centre streets. It raises funds for local charities, including the Sue Ryder Hospice at Leckhampton.

Gloucester Pirate Walk

Alongside Gloucester's Tall Ships Festival and Sea Shanty Festival, pirates of all sizes and ages take part in the city's Pirate Walk, also organised by Café Rene. It is a lively dressed-up jaunt around the city centre raising vital funds for the Severn Area Rescue Association.

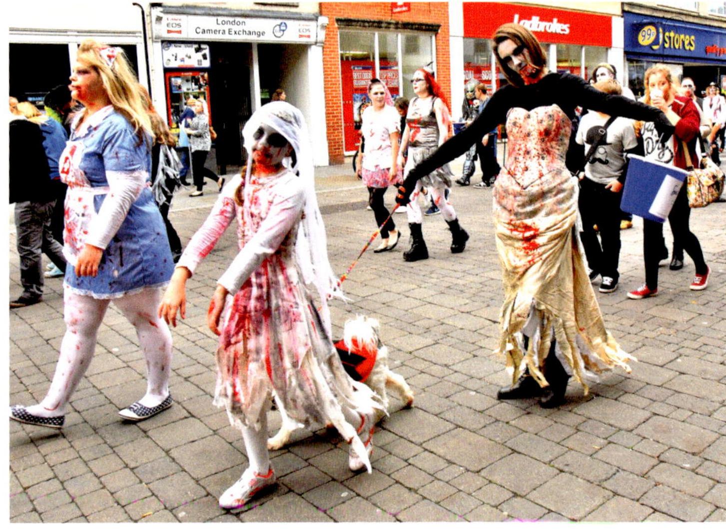

Gloucester's Zombie Walk makes its way through the city centre. (Roger Smith)

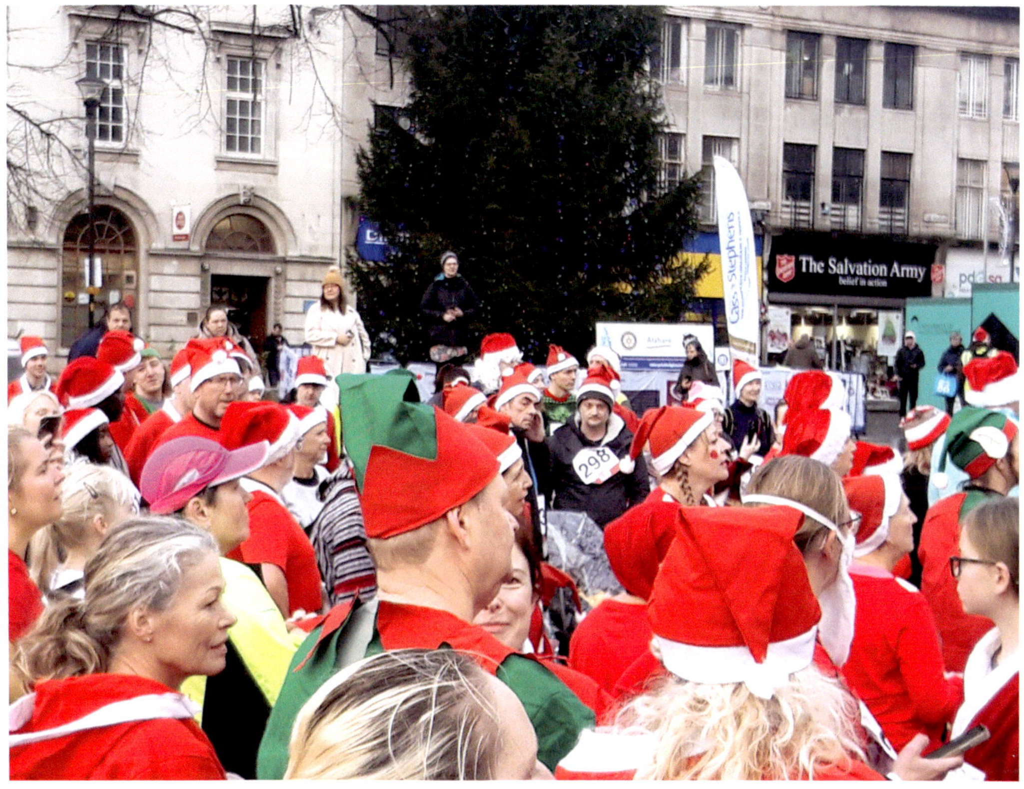

Crowds gather for the Santa Fun Run, which sets off from Kings Square.

Gloucester Santa Fun Run

Organised by the Rotary Club of Gloucester, the city's Santa Fun Run has grown since it was first introduced in 2018.

Many hundreds of runners dressed as Santa and in other festive costumes gather in Kings Square and run either a 1 km or 5 km route around the city centre streets on the second Saturday in December. The event has raised many thousands of pounds for local charities.

Gloucester as a Film Location

These days Gloucester is a popular film location – most famously for a number of Harry Potter films, where Gloucester Cathedral's magnificent cloisters appeared as part of Hogwarts School of Witchcraft and Wizardry.

Everything had to look just perfect, so the geniuses from Warner Brothers avoided audiences seeing some ugly-looking wires and switches, which would have detracted from the otherwise splendid setting, by covering them with a wooden box painted in stone effect. Cathedral bosses liked the look so much that they left it in place and it is now forever-known as the 'Harry Potter Box'!

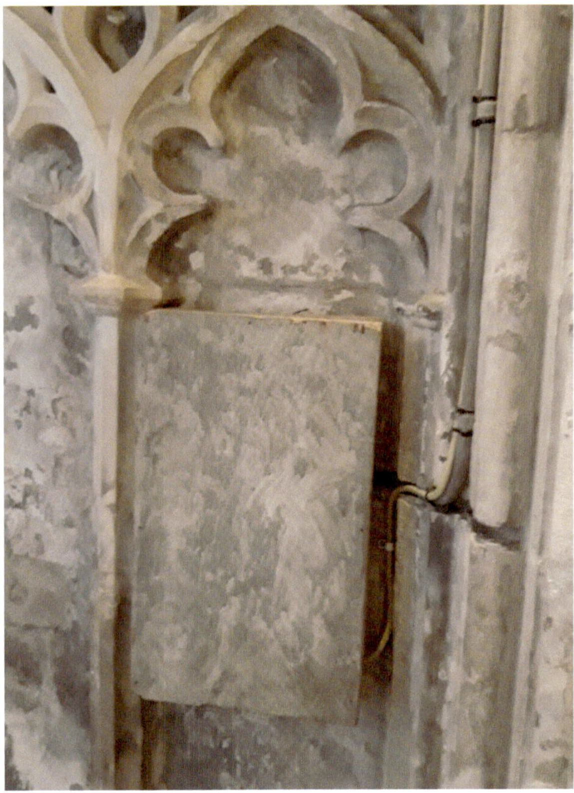

The 'Harry Potter' box at Gloucester Cathedral.

Another well-known film shoot that took place in Gloucester was *Alice Through the Looking Glass*, which was filmed at Gloucester Docks. The newly renovated Victorian warehouses were dressed to represent London in the 1850s.

The production took over the Docks for a week with Mia Wasikowska playing Alice and Johnny Depp playing the Mad Hatter (although it is believed Johnny didn't come to Gloucester). The production featured 300 crew, 150 extras, forty technical vehicles, eighteen horses, five magnificent tall ships and two llamas!

Peter Rabbit 2: The Runaway, released in 2020, had much of the story based in Gloucester, but only a small amount (shots of the cathedral and the Docks) was filmed here. The iconic House of the Tailor of Gloucester in College Court was recreated on location in Australia. Eagle-eyed viewers will have noticed that there was a parking space alongside the shop in the film – but, of course, that doesn't exist next to the real building. Peter Rabbit and his friends run rampage in the Farmer's Market in Gloucester in the film, which took place in a square on a Saturday. In real life, Gloucester's Farmer's Market takes place on The Cross on Fridays.

Perhaps lesser-known is the filming of *Outlaw*, an action-thriller which was released in 2007 but was filmed in Gloucester in 2006. Two of the stars, Sean Bean and Danny Dyer, filmed a scene inside a white transit van parked in the Land Registry car park just off Bruton Way in the city centre!

Unusual Buildings, Places and Features

Hillfield House

The most expensive, and probably the largest, house to come to the market in recent times was the eight-bed Hillfield House on Denmark Road, which has twenty-three rooms, including a 'Tower Room', and several stained-glass windows. It was the former offices of the County Council's Trading Standards department before being painstakingly restored to a family home by its previous owners. It came onto the market for £1.85 million in 2020, and sold for £1.5 million according to Land Registry records. It later went back on the market for £2 million and was bought by the Diocese of Gloucester in 2024 to convert back to offices.

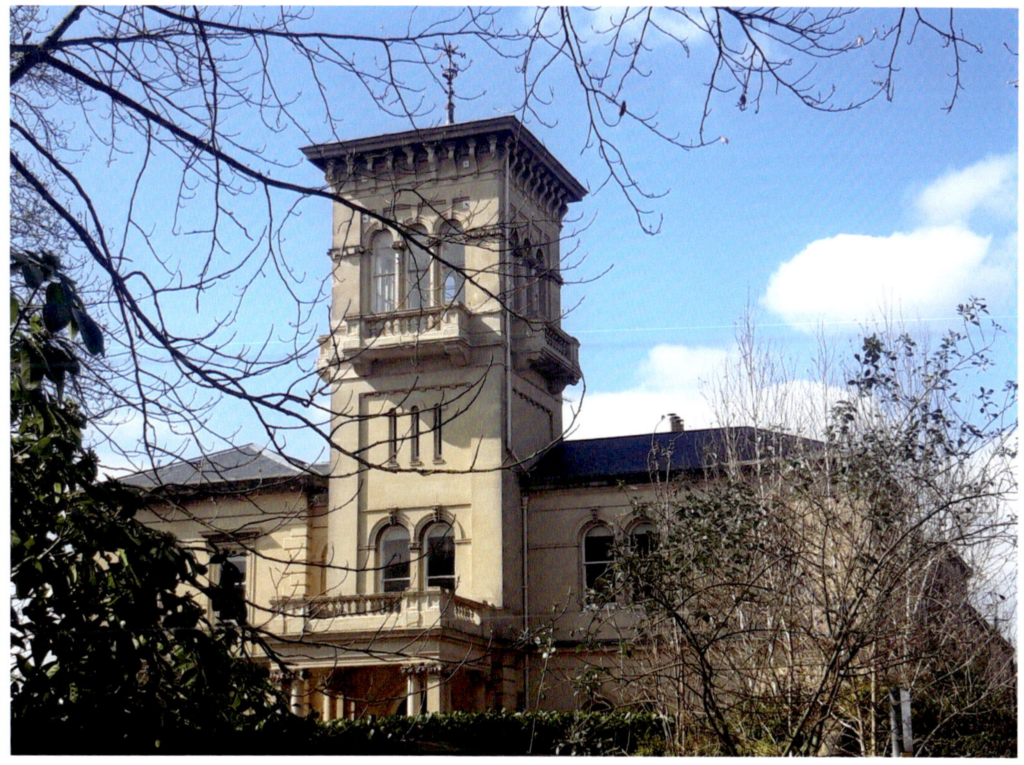

Hillfield House in Denmark Road.

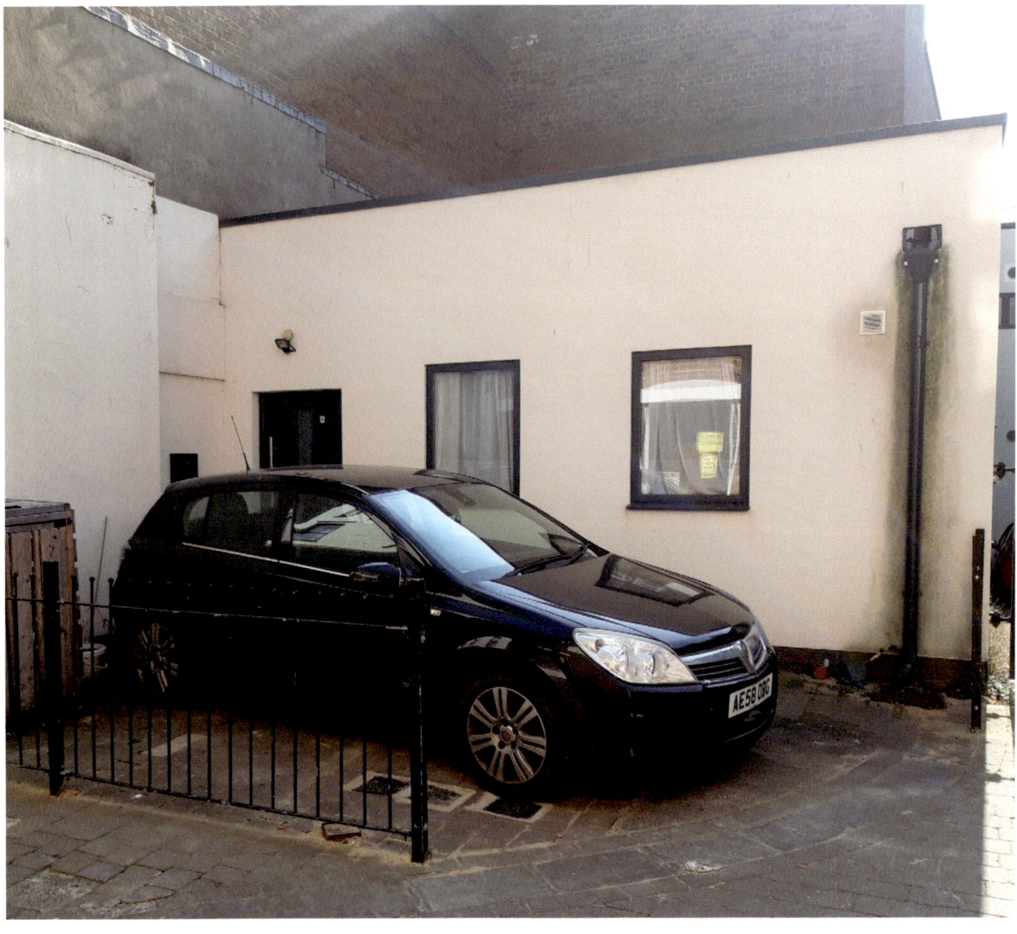

The former public toilets in St John's Lane – now a dwelling.

Former Toilets, St John's Lane

Probably the smallest standalone dwelling to be created in the city is the former gents' toilets in St John's Lane in the city centre. A planning application was submitted in 2018 to turn the 1970s block into a one-bedroom house and work was subsequently carried out to convert the building.

Addison's Folly

Tucked away by the Greyfriars monument and Café René pub is Addison's Folly, sometimes known as Addison House. Built as a memorial to Robert Raikes in 1864 by Thomas Fenn Addison, the tower was designed so that he could view Hempsted Church (1.5 miles away), where his wife, Hannah, was buried. It has been used as offices in the past but has been empty for many years. There are plans to turn it into serviced apartments as part of the redevelopment of the Eastgate Shopping Centre and Indoor Market.

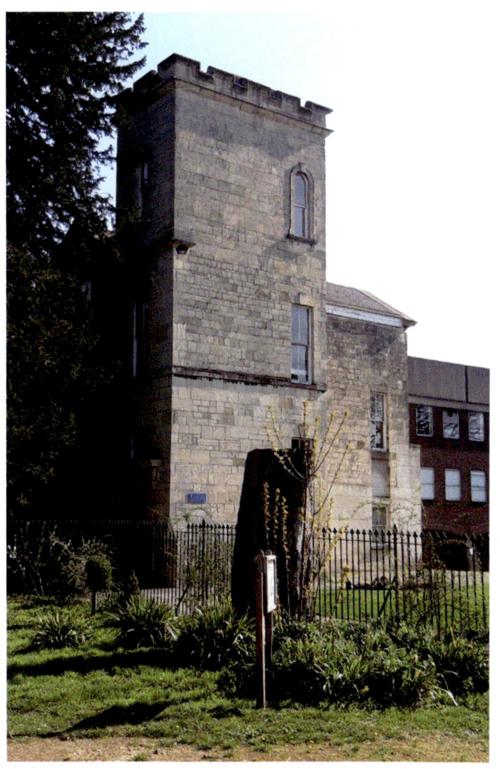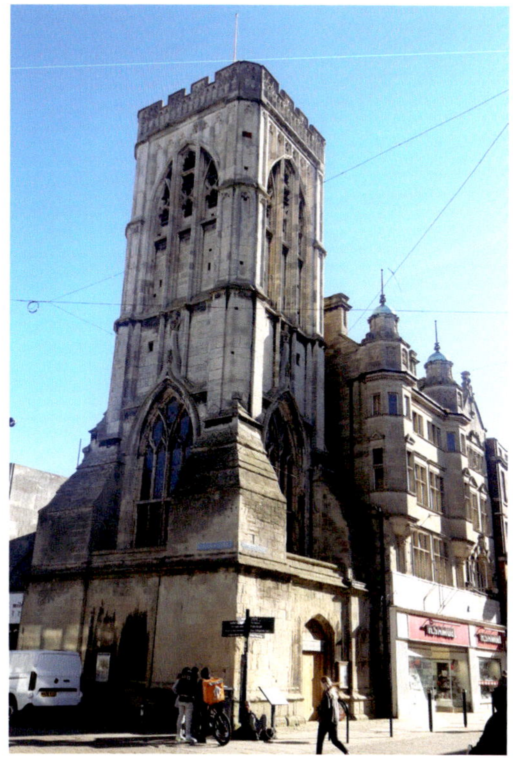

Above left: Addison's Folly in the Greyfriars area of the city.

Above right: St Michael's Tower.

St Michael's Tower

St Michael's Tower, on Gloucester Cross, was built in 1465 on the site of the nave of the previous church of St Michael the Archangel. There has been a church on the site since the twelfth century. Its bells were rung to signal the curfew imposed on citizens to extinguish their home fires overnight. This was especially important as most of the city's buildings were made from timber.

In the 1840s the old church was demolished, apart from the tower, and a new church was constructed in 1851. The new church closed in 1940 and the main part of the new church was demolished in 1956, but again the tower was spared. For a number of years it was used as the city's Tourist Information Centre, but was taken on and restored by Gloucester Civic Trust and is now used as a heritage centre.

Baker's Jewellers

Above the beautifully preserved Edwardian shopfront of Baker's Jewellers in Southgate Street is a chiming clock built in 1904 by Niehus Brothers of Bristol. The bells are struck on the quarter hour by the figures of Old Father Time, John

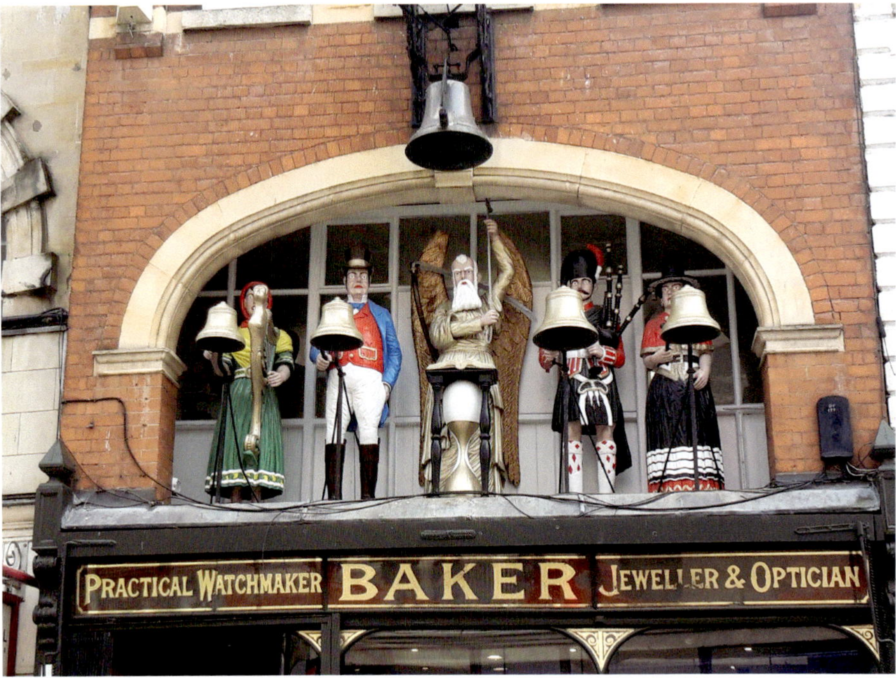

Figures at Baker's Jewellers in Southgate Street.

Bull representing England and other 'striking' figures wearing the national dress for Ireland, Scotland and Wales.

Our Lady's Well, Hempsted

Our Lady's Well can be found hidden away in a field in Hempsted. It has been described as being 'one of the most interesting and picturesquely-placed holy wells in Gloucestershire', despite being located near to a former landfill site. The well house

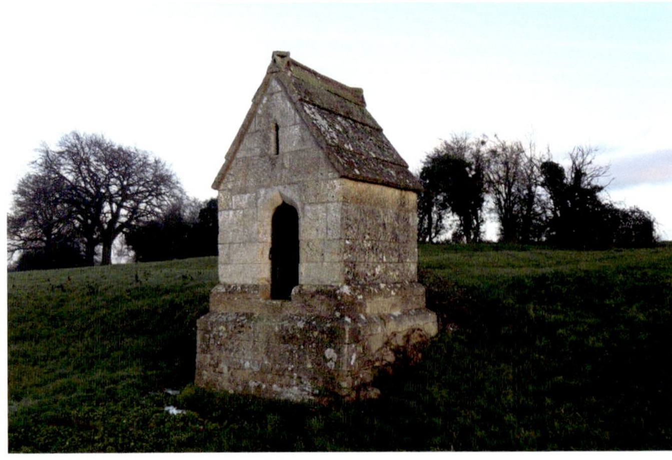

Our Lady's Well in Hempsted.

was built in the fourteenth century for the Manor of Hempsted, which was held by Llanthony Secunda Priory. The well house is a tall structure built from limestone blocks with an arched opening at the front. Water comes from the front into a large stone trough, with a rectangular water trough added in the eighteenth or nineteenth century, which would have provided water for livestock. On the back of the well is a stone sculpture showing St Anne standing between her daughter, the virgin Mary, and an angel. It has been used as a baptistery, and formerly was considered to have medicinal properties. In the past it has been a place for pilgrimage, with numerous pilgrims being recorded as coming to the site to seek cures. Pilgrimage was revived in 1989 for several years but has now long since stopped.

Gloucester Prison

The Victorian block of Gloucester Prison has some quirky features, including the brackets used to hold up the floors outside the cells. Each bracket is a sinuous snake complete with scales and eyes. The serpent represents evil in Victorian symbology. Above each one, on the floor above, the base of the balustrade is

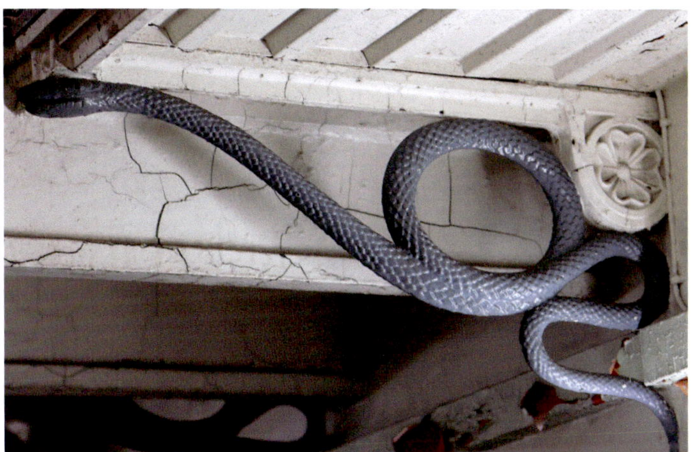

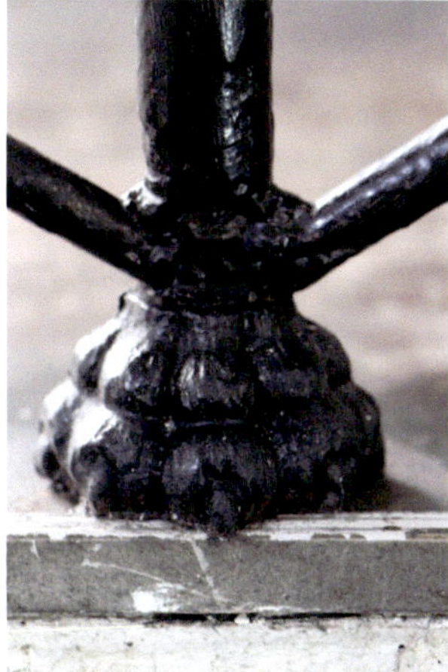

Above left: A snake figure at Gloucester Prison. (Clive Barzillia)

Above right: A lion's paw at Gloucester Prison. (Clive Barzillia)

Right: Graffiti carved into the wall of the Debtors' Prison building at Gloucester Prison. (Clive Barzillia)

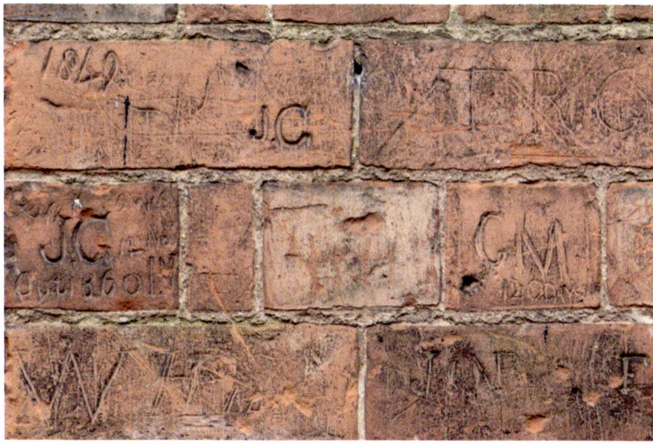

a lion's paw. The lion's paw represents strength and character. The meaning is clear – a simple 'good overcoming evil' message to the inhabitants of the prison, strength overcoming weakness and vice.

The wall of the Debtors' Prison building, built in 1826, within the site has graffiti of initials carved by prisoners over the centuries (see photo).

The prison closed in 2013 and, despite being granted planning permission for a development of over 200 apartments, remains largely unchanged at the time of writing. Various activities take place on the site, including tours, ghost hunts, airsoft, wrestling and it has been used several times as a film location.

Gloucester Cathedral Solar Panels

In November 2016, 150 solar panels were installed by local firm Mypower on the south side of the nave roof. They generate around 29,000 kW of energy every year or over a quarter of the cathedral's electricity needs. This initiative made Gloucester it the first ancient cathedral, the oldest building in the country and the oldest cathedral in the world to have solar panels fitted.

Never one to miss a PR opportunity, the Dean at the time, the Very Reverend Stephen Lake, blessed the panels, wearing full robes, on the regional television news and the cathedral's famous tower was illuminated green in celebration.

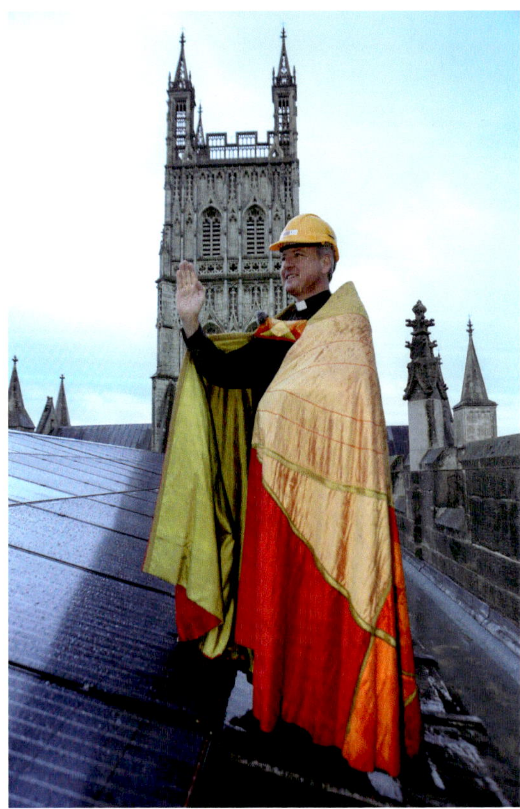

Stephen Lake, then Dean of Gloucester, blessing newly installed solar panels on the roof of Gloucester Cathedral. (Gloucester Cathedral)

Gloucester Cathedral Gargoyles

In 2019, six new gargoyles were added at Gloucester Cathedral to channel rainwater off the roof. They represent the six districts of the county: Gloucester, Cheltenham, Tewkesbury, Stroud, Cotswold and the Forest of Dean. Each gargoyle was designed by Master Mason Pascal Mychalysin. The designs are a Gloucester rugby player, a Cheltenham jockey, a Cooper's Hill cheese-rolling contestant (representing Tewkesbury Borough), a Stroud Mills suffragette, a Cotswold sheep shearer and Forest of Dean Freeminer. The rugby player gargoyle – called Glaaaawster – has cauliflower ears and is clutching a ball. It can be found, fittingly, on the North Ambulatory roof, overlooking Kingsholm Stadium.

Gloucester's Roman City Wall

Despite the best efforts of King Charles II, parts of Gloucester's Roman city wall still remain. Perhaps the quirkiest example is in a long-established furniture store in the city's Southgate Street. The owners are happy for members of the public to call in to view it and indeed it forms part of Gloucester Civic Trust's city tours. A sign on display in the store states that this section of wall is 'the oldest Roman masonry in Britain – as it was erected by Vespasian while commanding the second Legion in the middle of the first century'.

Other parts of the city wall can be found in the Museum of Gloucester and outside Boots in Eastgate Street.

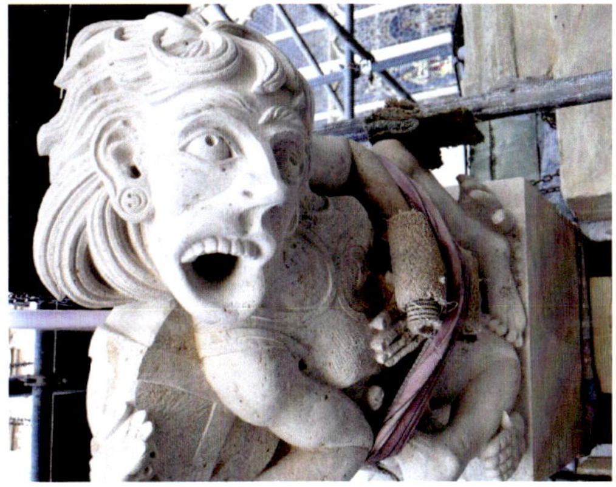

Above: The cheese-roller gargoyle at Gloucester Cathedral. (Gloucester Cathedral)

Right: The Roman city wall on display in the Gloucester Furniture store in Southgate Street.

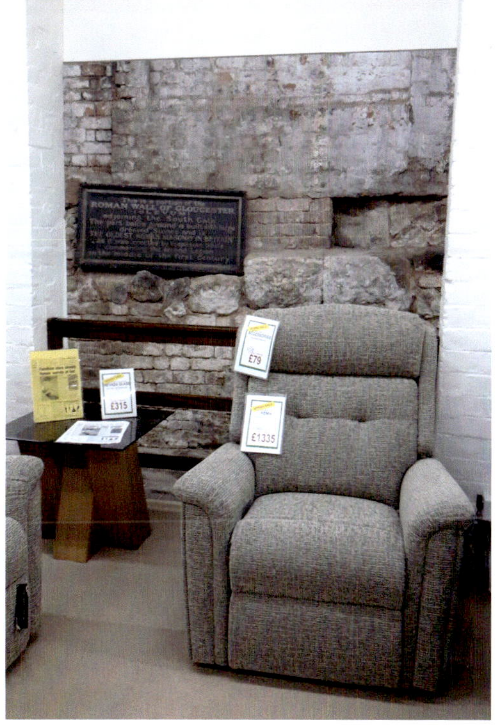

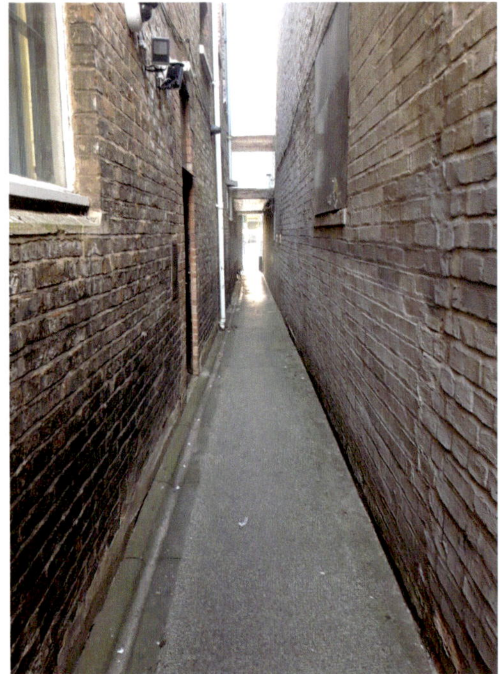

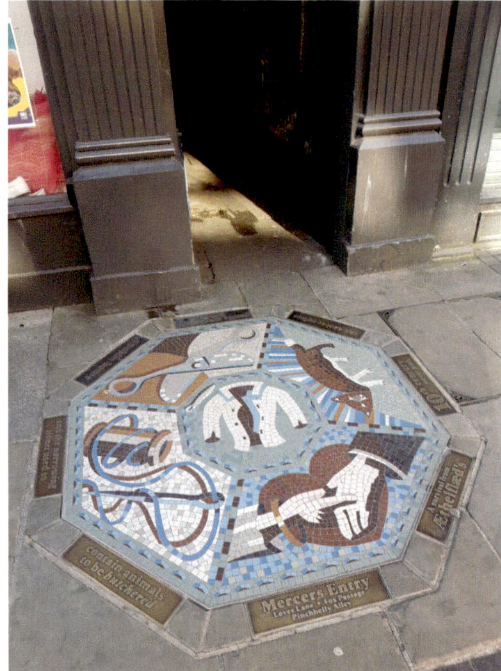

Above left: Pinchbelly Alley looking towards Westgate Street.

Above right: A mosaic on the Westgate Street entrance to Pinchbelly Alley.

Pinchbelly Alley

Pinchbelly Alley, off Westgate Street, is the last remaining tenth-century side street still in public use in Gloucester. It was named Pinchbelly Alley as it had two stones placed to stop animals rushing through. The stones and the old medieval wall are still visible. It has been known by other names over the years including Mercers Entry (associated with the cloth trade), Lovers Lane (which doesn't take too much imagination to work out) and Fox Passage.

26 Westgate Street

This property is situated on the corner of Westgate Street and Maverdine Lane. Looking at the nineteenth-century frontage, you could be totally unaware of what lies behind. A clue to the history of the lane and the house can be found in the mosaic at the entrance to the lane, put there in more recent times to celebrate the heritage of the city.

The property is a fusion of four different ages: medieval, Tudor, Georgian and twentieth century. The oldest part of the building dates to 1470. The internationally recognised Tudor part was constructed around 1540. In the late eighteenth century these two houses were joined together, extended to the rear, and upwards to the attic. Being a grand property, situated on Westgate Street, which was one of the most important streets in England because much traffic heading in and out of Wales came through it, I'm told it was like the Trump Tower of its day!

The building has, during its history of more than 500 years, been a merchant's town house, an apothecary, a merchants' guild and a clothier. For more than 120 years it was home to Winfields seed merchants. It featured on Griff Rhys Jones' television programme *Britain's Lost Routes* in 2012.

Since 2015 it has been home to the Gloucester Antiques Centre, which relocated from Gloucester Quays. The centre is home to around forty different dealers, who trade in everything from stamps, coins, cigarette cards, jewellery, toys, clothing and memorabilia. It is packed full with literally hundreds of thousands of items across several higgledy-piggledy floors. The different levels are linked by what traders call their 'burglar stairs' – stairs which are uneven and would lead to someone unfamiliar with the building who was in a hurry being likely to come a cropper!

Over the years, it has seen some unusual items. Some collectors of uranium glass objects have been known to wander round the centre with a Geiger counter to test the radiation in the said items. One visitor travelled from North Wales to ask for a valuation of a Hadrosaur (dinosaur) egg – and was told they'd be better taking it to a museum. A few years ago, a dealer sold an antique dentistry set, including fragments of false teeth, as a Christmas present for a retired dentist. And apparently Edwardian enema kits have also been a popular line!

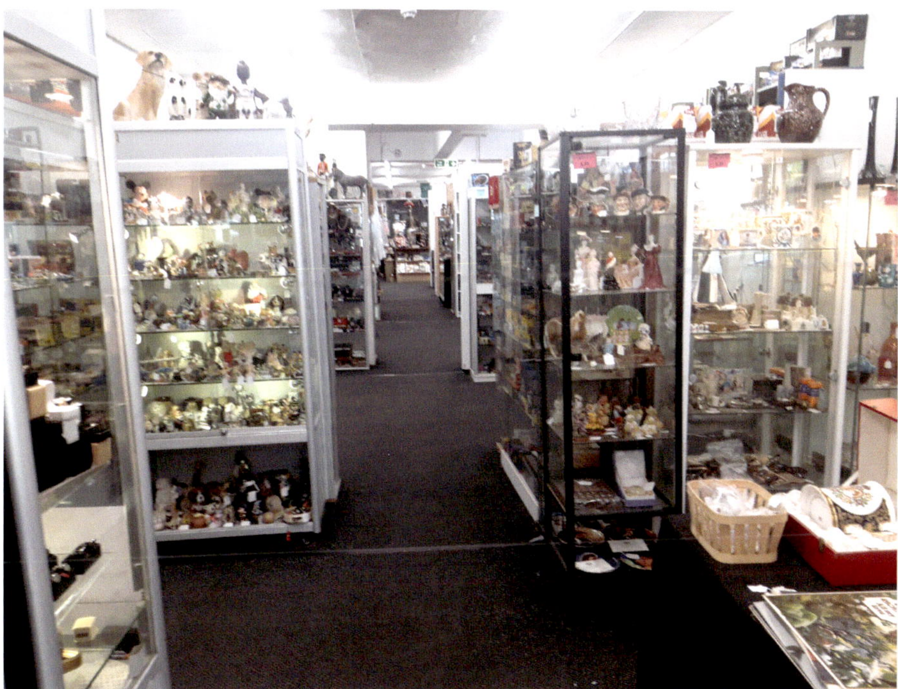

Inside the Aladdin's Cave of the Gloucester Antiques Centre.

Eastgate Portico

The portico at the Eastgate Street entrance to the Eastgate Shopping Centre is an example of Greek Revivalist architecture.

The portico and its large Corinthian columns were built in 1856. The arches were moved to their current location in 1973, having been originally located slightly further up Eastgate Street towards The Cross, at the entrance to the then Eastgate Market.

It features Father Time on the right and Ceres (the goddess of harvest) on the left. At the feet of both figures can be seen some realistically carved market produce.

Bearland Lodge

This town house, now offices, was built around 1720 for William Lane, a barrister. It has a very ornate feature at its apex. In the centre is the figure of Perseus (a Greek hero), in a billowing cloak and wearing a helmet, sitting on the back of a lion with a winged cherub to the right, a staff in his left hand and, in his right hand, his shield reflecting the head of the Medusa.

Lampkin House, 1 Commercial Road

Built in around 1849 as the Gloucester Savings Bank, this building has now been converted to flats. It is distinguished by a series of carved faces above the ground-floor windows, which are in remarkably good condition.

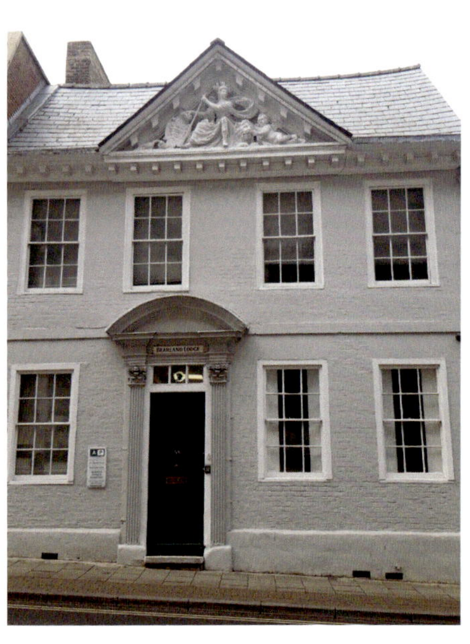

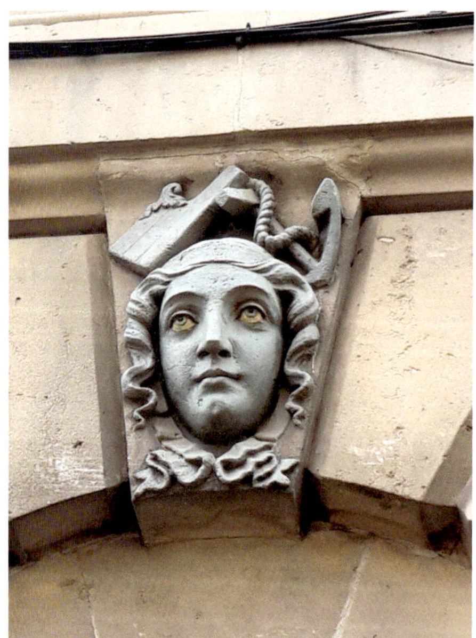

Above left: Bearland Lodge.

Above right: One of the carved faces at Lampkin House.

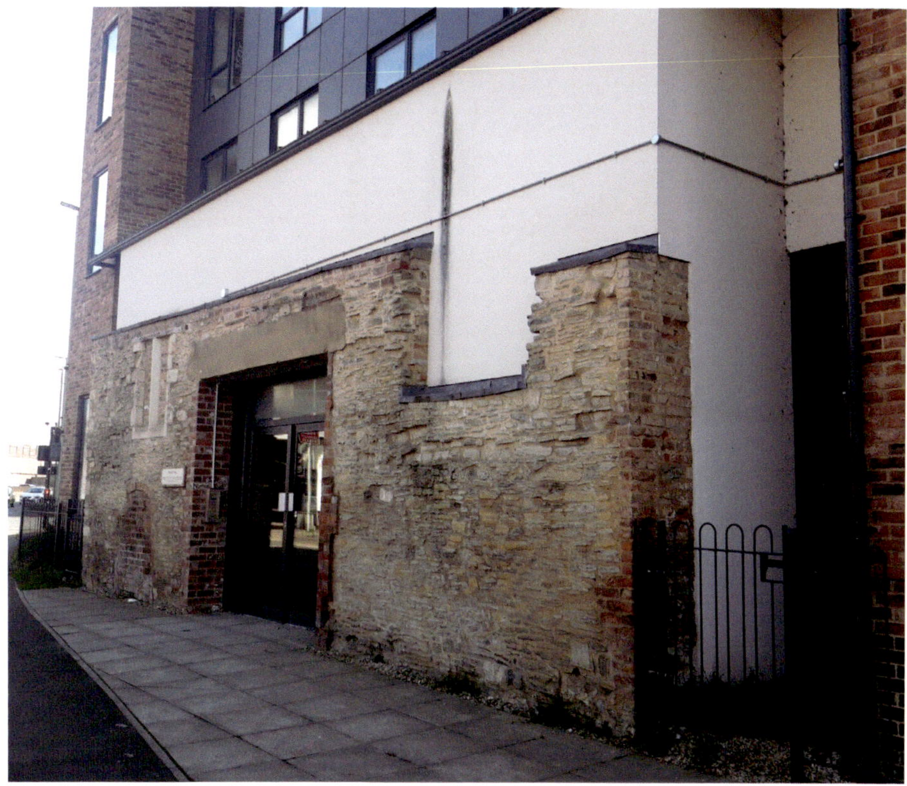

The remains of the Tanner's Hall, incorporated into a new development of flats.

Tanners Hall, Gouda Way

Tanners Hall is the oldest non-religious building and only surviving medieval domestic stone house in the city. A new apartment block, built by Cape Homes, sensitively incorporates the surviving remains of this thirteenth-century medieval town house used by the Company of Tanners, one of the oldest craft organisations in the city. The preserved walls have been cleverly incorporated into the ground floor and accentuated by light from the windows above, resulting in a unique and impressive lobby.

The Oxebode

The Oxebode in the city centre was known as Oxbody Lane, which was first recorded in 1263, and at times has also been known as Mitre Street. In medieval times, it was lined by houses that leaned towards each other on either side and were almost touching at the end of the street as it led into Northgate Street. In fact, the funnel was so narrow that an ox being led to market became wedged solid between the houses and could not be freed. A local butcher was summoned to kill the ox where it stood and cut it up into pieces of meat that were then sold to the local populace.

The event led to the street being renamed Oxbody Street and to a local nursery rhyme:

There's an ox lying dead at the end of the lane
His head on the pathway, his feet in the drain.
The lane is so narrow, his back is so wide,
He got stuck in the road 'twixt a house on each side.

He couldn't go forward, he couldn't go back
He was stuck just as fast as a nail in a crack.
And the people all shouted 'So tightly he fits
We must kill him and carve him and move him in bits.'

So a butcher dispatched him and then had a sale
Of his ribs and his sirloin, his rump and his tail.
And the farmer he told me 'I'll never again
Drive cattle to market down Oxbody Lane.'

Over the years, Oxbody Lane became corrupted to The Oxebode. The area was cleared of slum houses in the 1920s and the existing shopping area was built in 1929.

Denmark Road Dalek

It has today been claimed that the inspiration behind one of science fiction's most fearsome characters was a simple chimney pot from a school in Gloucester.

BBC designer Raymond Cusick is believed to have created Doctor Who's most evil nemesis, the Daleks, after seeing the design at the High School for Girls (now known as Denmark Road High School) in the city during a visit to Gloucester in the 1960s.

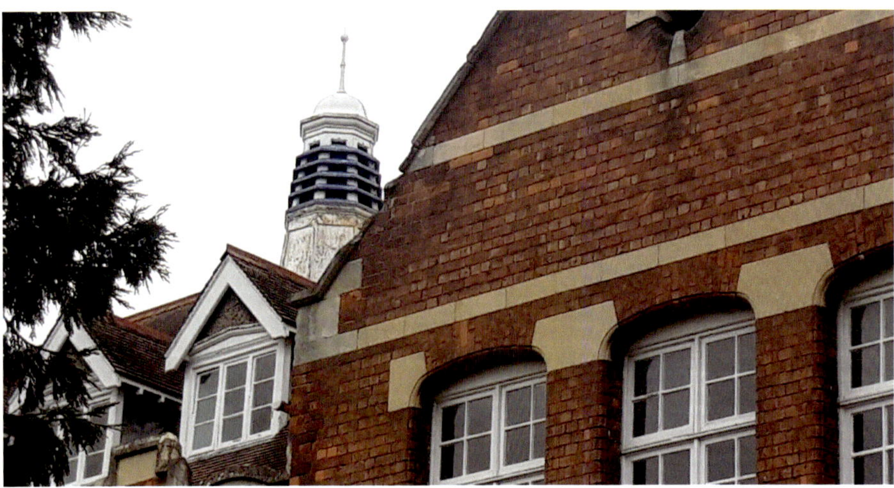

The 'Dalek' on the roof of Denmark Road High School.

Café René

Café René, a popular pub in the Greyfriars area of the city centre, has many historic features, including an authentic Roman well in the bar. In addition to this, the restaurant area used to be an old stable, and is now lined with old wine bottles, giving a unique feel to the room. The well came into its own during the floods of summer 2007, enabling the pub to stay open even when the water supply to the city was lost.

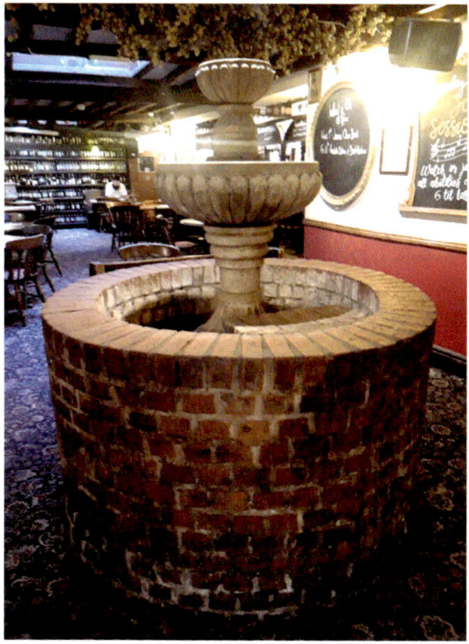

Right: The Roman well in Café René.

Below: The unusual ceiling made of wine bottles at Café René.

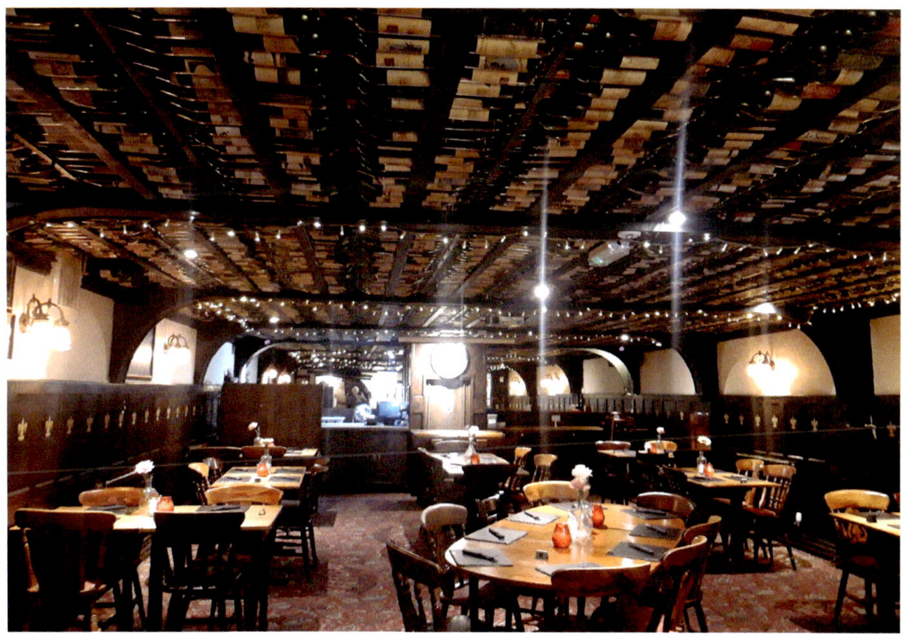

Tunnels

Does Gloucester have a vast underground network beneath itself dating back centuries? It's a question that has inspired many a debate in the city over the years with the full truth not really known.

The *Daily Express* reported in November 2023 that a sinkhole that appeared on a residential road in the city could be linked to a network of underground tunnels. It was claimed that the network could extend to 22 miles of tunnels!

One of the sites most frequently spoken about is the Monks' Retreat underground bar at the currently mothballed Fleece Hotel. This tunnel is said to have run from Llanthony Priory to the abbey (now the cathedral) – which would be quite a feat of engineering!

Other underground tunnels are said to run to and from buildings including Café René, The Cavern (formerly The Services Club in College Street) and Mark Blake hairdressers in Westgate Street.

Gloucester Food Dock

Behind the Bella Mia pizza restaurant in Gloucester Food Dock is a 'secret' cocktail bar. It sits behind a sliding green door with a secret mirrored window and includes a reclaimed oak floor from the original set of the 1964 *Mary Poppins* film, which was brought to Gloucester from Westminster.

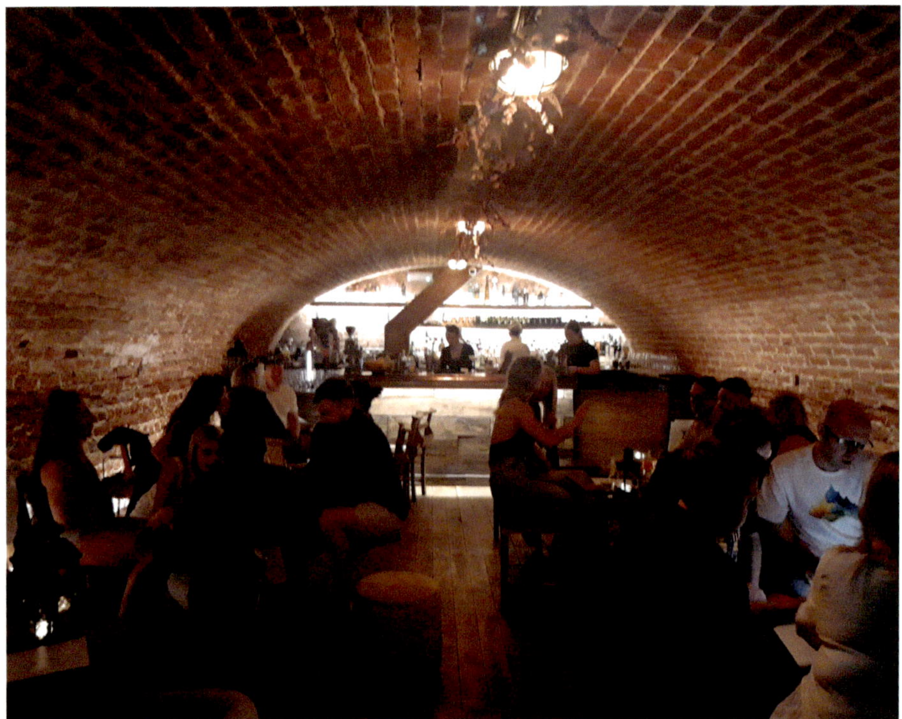

The Green Door cocktail bar at Gloucester Docks.

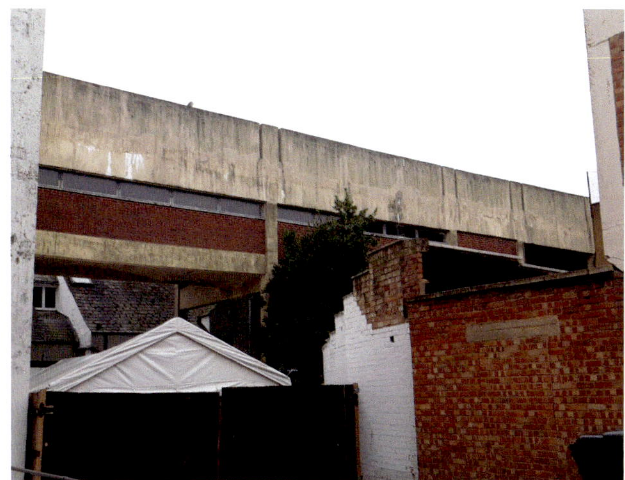

The remains of the bridge which used to link Longsmith Street car parks to other multi-storey car parks in the city centre.

Gloucester's Car Park Super High-way

After the city centre development of the 1970s, the rooftop car parks at Eastgate and Kings Walk and the multi-storey car park at Longsmith Street were all linked via bridges over Eastgate Street and Southgate Street – meaning you could easily drive from one to another if you couldn't find a space!

The bridge link across Southgate Street to the Longsmith Street car park was largely demolished in the 1990s, but a part remains, near to the Cross Keys pub in Cross Keys Lane. The bridge across Eastgate Street remains but vehicles are no longer allowed to drive over it. For many years it was the studios for the Severn Sound radio station (later known as Heart) and, at the time of writing, is the City Council's offices.

There is also a rooftop car park on the top of what was The Chambers pub in Kings Square – but nobody ever got round to building an access to it!

A Rainbow City

Gloucester has built a reputation as a 'rainbow city' following a multi-year campaign by local student landlord Tash Frootko.

Starting off in Nettleton Road, in the city centre, Tash persuaded property owners to paint their houses in bright colours, with Tash co-ordinating the work. It had the effect of getting neighbours who hadn't really spoken before to talk to each other.

After Nettleton Road, Tash moved onto two roads in Kingsholm – Sebert Street and St Mark Street – before going back to St Kilda Parade and Station Road to turn the original rainbow street into a rainbow square.

She then switched her efforts to the Tredworth area, initially in Hopewell Street and then her biggest project to date – Tredworth's High Street. This project didn't just involve painting houses in vivid colours; it included a number of whacky murals, including a wall of cats and another featuring fruit and others with birds, foxes and what must be the country's (if not the world's) most brightly decorated takeaway chicken shop!

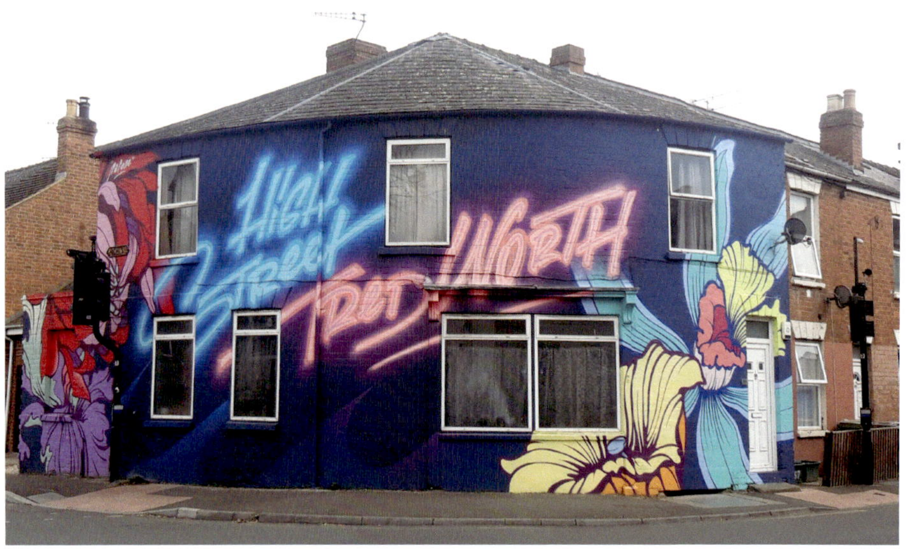

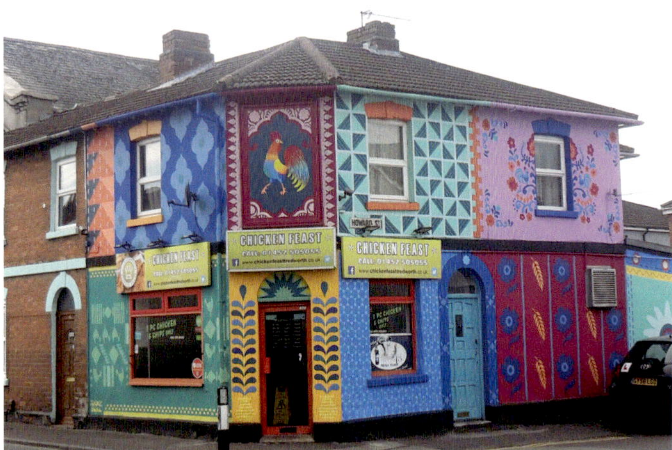

Above, left, below and opposite above: Some of the brightly coloured murals on properties in High Street, Tredworth.

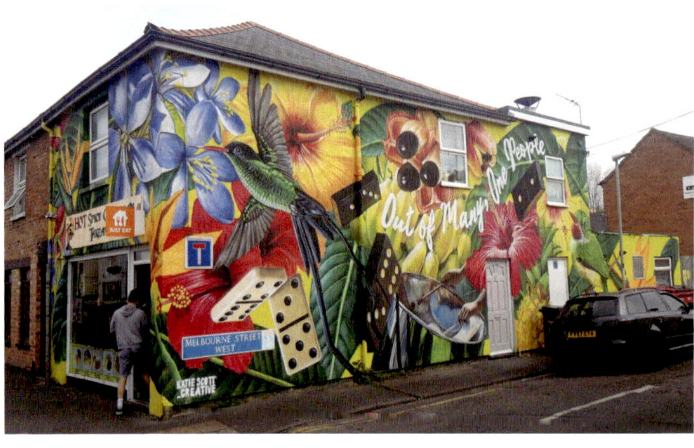

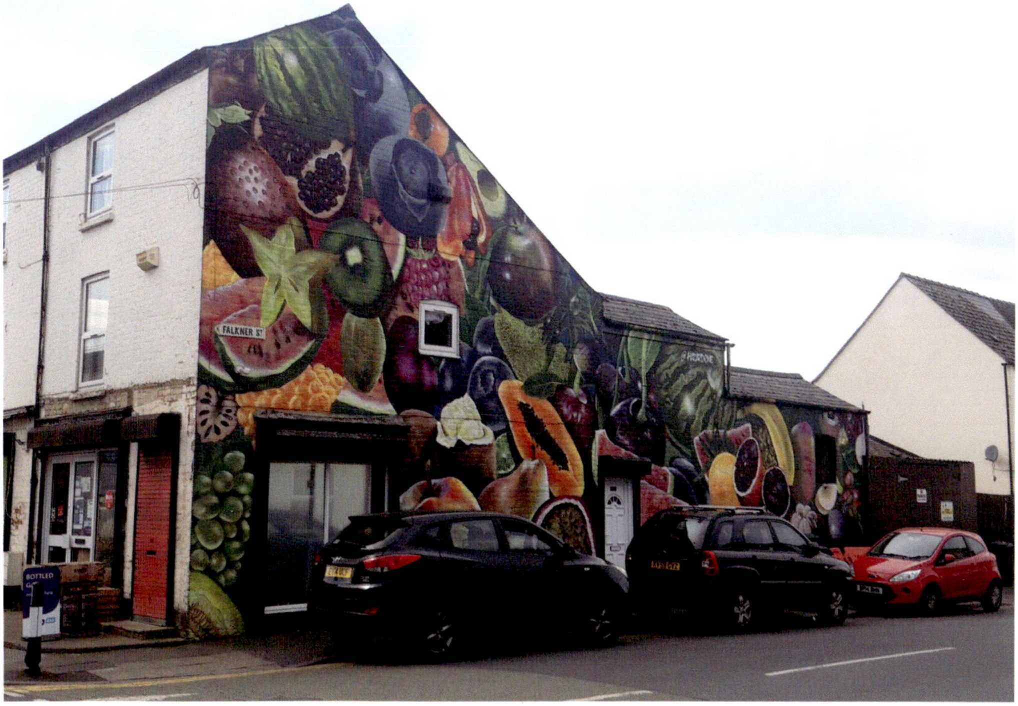

Below: The 'Rainbow Crossing' on Commercial Road.

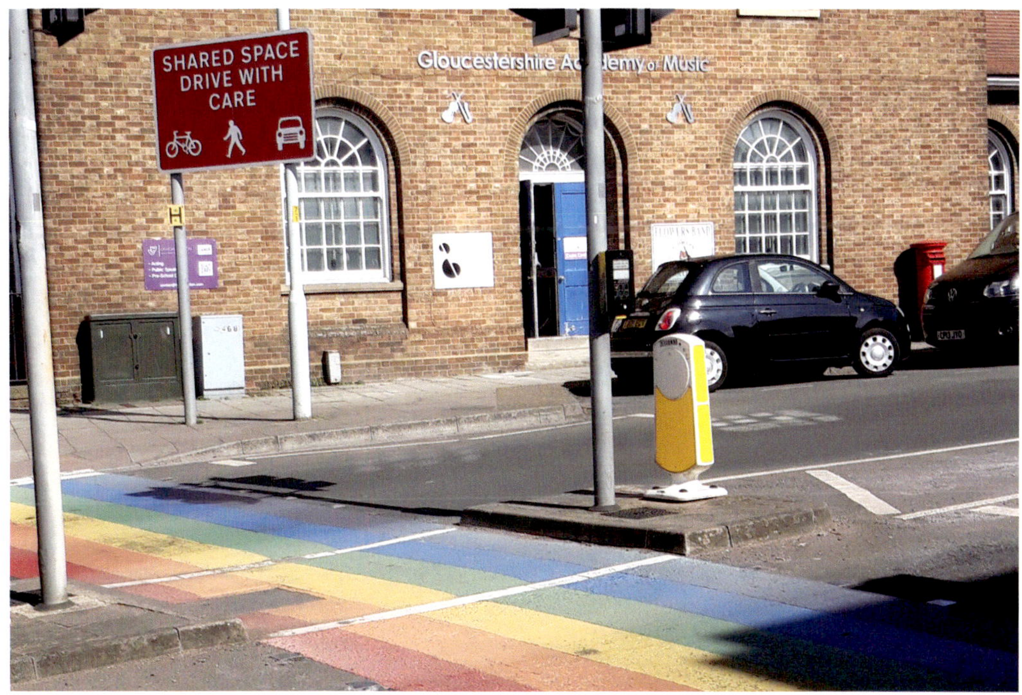

Tash's project has gained publicity nationally and all around the world. Another example of a rainbow feature in the city is the rainbow crossing on Commercial Road near the Docks. Installed in April 2021, it was described by the County Council as 'a small but inclusive contribution to celebrating our diverse communities'.

Leisure Centre Water Slides

Two new slides (known as Turbo Twisters) were brought in to halt the decline in swimming numbers. They were named 'Dolphin' (which was 83 metres long) and 'Stingray' (which was 72 metres long). They were installed by contractors C. H. Pearce at a cost of £500,000 and were officially opened on 23 May 1987.

An auction of unwanted furniture and fittings from the centre took place when the Leisure Centre closed for a major rebuild in the late 1990s. It raised £25,000. The Pineapple water slide ended up in the garden of a house in Whiteway in Miserden, near Stroud.

The Lord High Constable and The Regal

The Lord High Constable pub, operated by Wetherspoons, in the Docks is one of the busiest public houses in the city, but few people know why it was given this unusual name.

The venue gets its name from Miles of Gloucester, who founded the nearby Llanthony Secunda Priory in 1136 and was the first Lord High Constable of

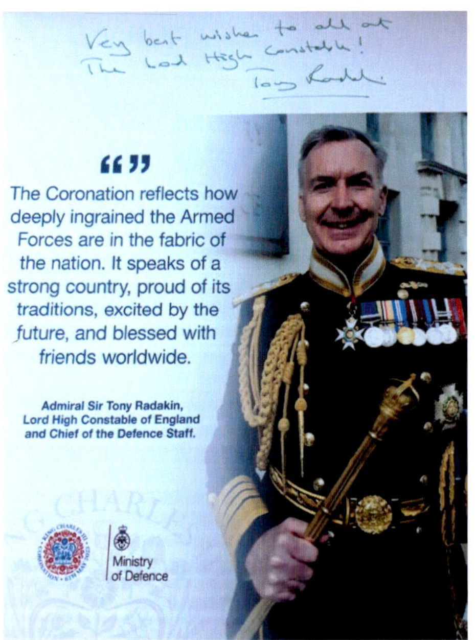

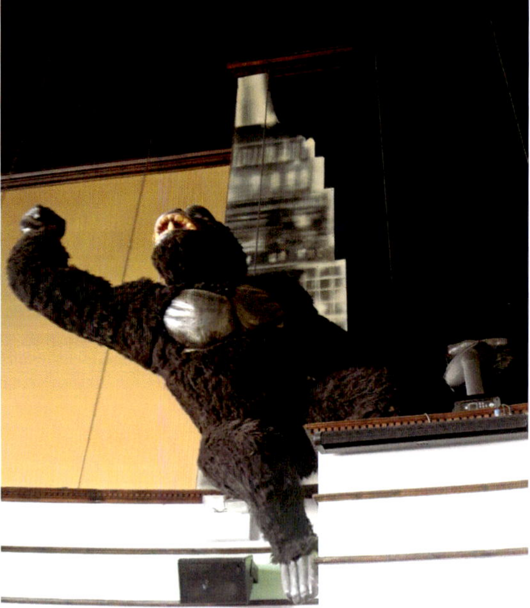

Above left: A message from the Lord High Constable to customers at the pub of the same name.

Above right: A large gorilla on display at The Regal pub in Gloucester.

England. The Lord High Constable of England is one of the Great Officers of State and at one point commanded the royal armies.

These days it is only called out of abeyance for coronations. The Chief of the Defence Staff, Admiral Sir Tony Radakin, performed the role at the Coronation of King Charles III in May 2023. In the pub, there is a framed print of a tweet posted by Admiral Sir Tony on Coronation Day which he has signed with a message to the pub's customers.

The other Wetherspoons pub in the city, The Regal in Kings Square, is well known as a former theatre and cinema; in fact, The Beatles performed there in March 1963. Various cinematic artefacts are dotted around the pub including a number of model biplanes, a couple of golden statuettes and a giant gorilla, along with a New York skyline filling the entire wall of the balcony that overlooks what was the auditorium.

Gloucester Services

The 'Gloucester Services' motorway service areas are located on both the northbound and southbound sides of the M5 between junctions 11a and 12. They are run by independent operator Westmorland, who operate the Tebay Services in Cumbria and promote local artisan produce. The service area supports the Gloucestershire Gateway Trust in assisting the business to provide good jobs for more deprived areas of Gloucester, and to support local social regeneration schemes.

It has a 4,000 sqm green roof which was designed to disguise the new service station as part of the landscape as it has the Cotswolds on one side and Robinswood Hill on the other. It won the Civic Voice Design Awards in 2015 and television presenter Griff Rhys Jones, as President of Civic Voice, launched the 2016 awards from the northbound services in December 2015.

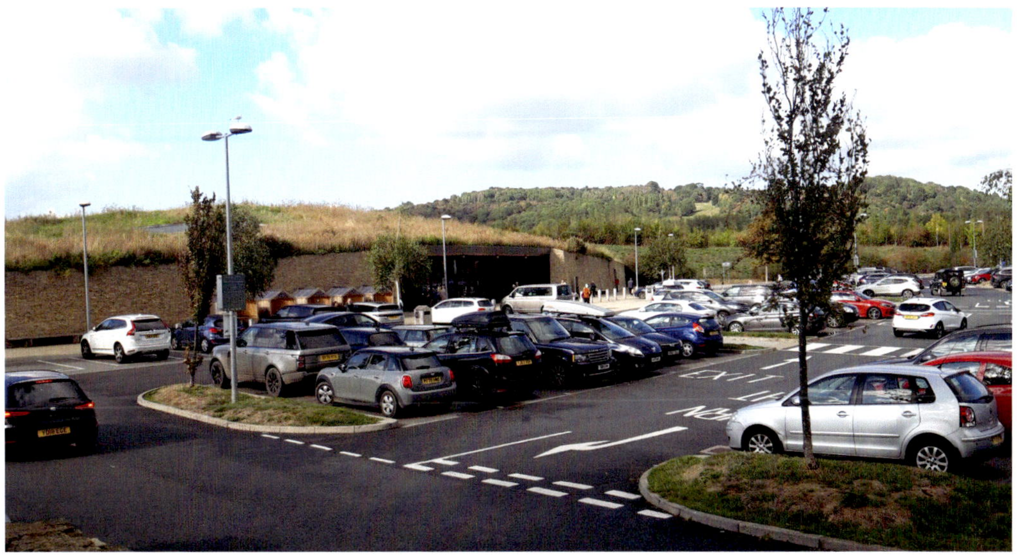

The Gloucester Services motorway service area on the M5.

Christmas Lights

Over the years, Gloucester has had more than its fair share of residents who have gone over and above to create Christmas light displays to wow visitors and raise money for charity.

Stuntman Dick Sheppard (qv) for many years had an amazing display at his home in Stroud Road, Tuffley, and raised over £40,000 for the Pied Piper Appeal.

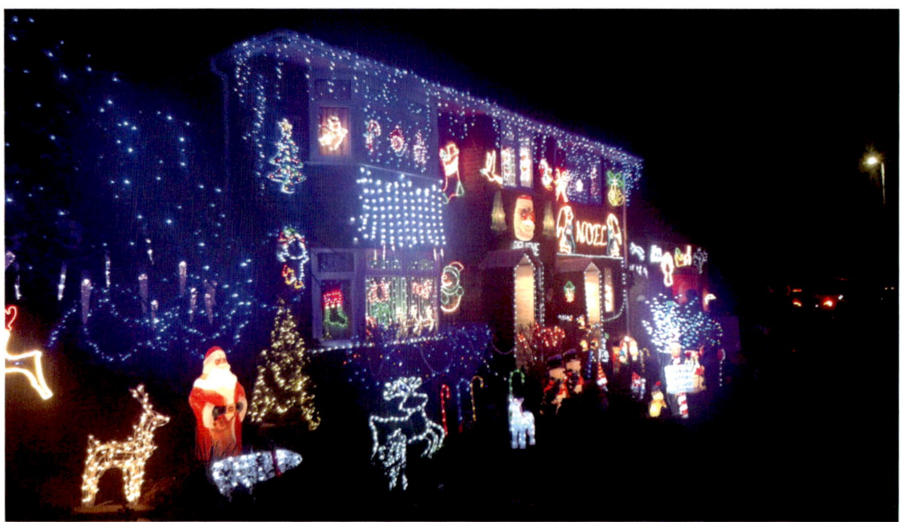

Christmas lights in Ogbourne Close, Longlevens.

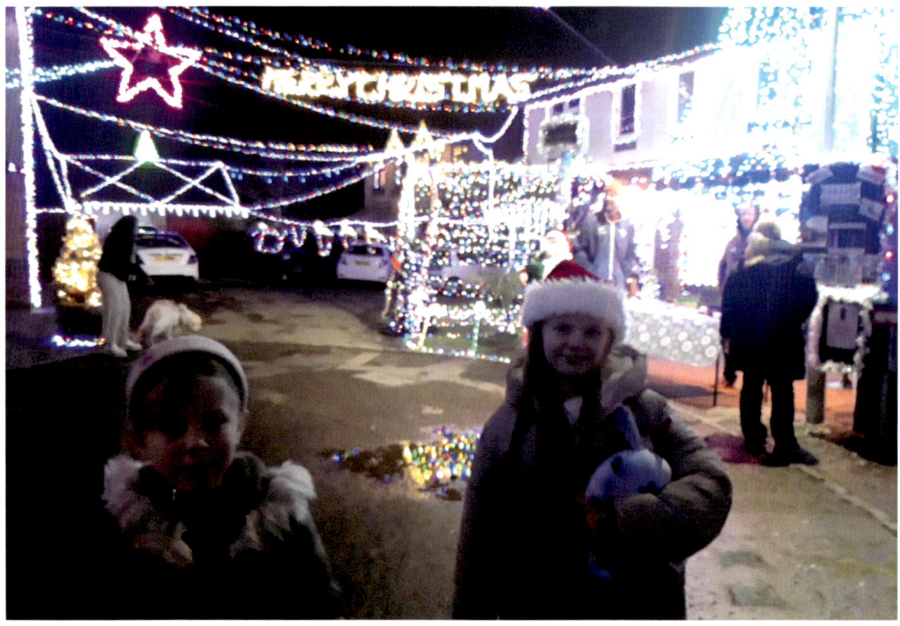

Christmas lights in Cotton Close, Abbeymead.

For over twenty years, Ernie and Josie Talbot brightened Ogbourne Close in Longlevens with their annual Christmas light display, raising money every year for a different charity.

In 2024, Brady Rogers and neighbours in Cotton Close, Abbeymead, came together to create their own remarkable display to spread some Christmas cheer to the community. They raised money for Great Western Air Ambulance and SMA (spinal muscular atrophy) because a young girl in the community was diagnosed with the condition after birth.

The Forum

Gloucester's long-awaited Forum development includes a couple of quirky features. A 'green wall' on the new multi-storey car park is designed to improve biodiversity, boost air quality and help with temperature control by cooling the building in the summer.

It is made up of more than 4,800 panels and 48,000 individual plants, set to capture the same amount of carbon as thirty-two trees. The plants are mostly evergreen with some bulbs providing splashes of seasonal colour. The plants spent two years growing in a nursery before being planted into the specially designed panels. They are watered through a hydroponics system running through the wall using a plant feed that includes recycled rainwater.

Intricate panels on the office buildings at the Forum take their inspiration from the world-famous Cloisters at Gloucester Cathedral.

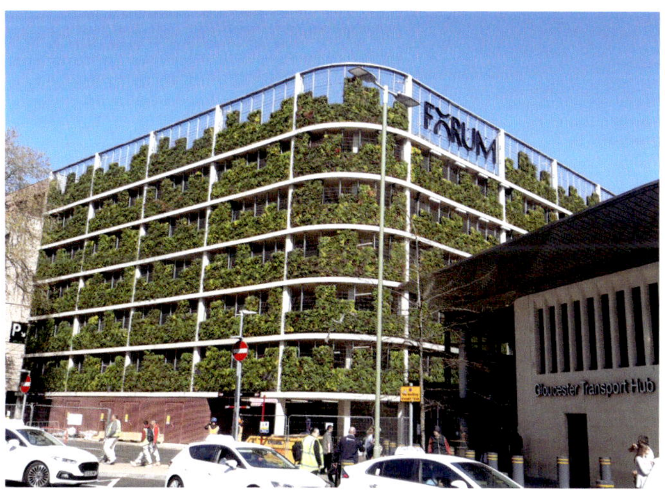

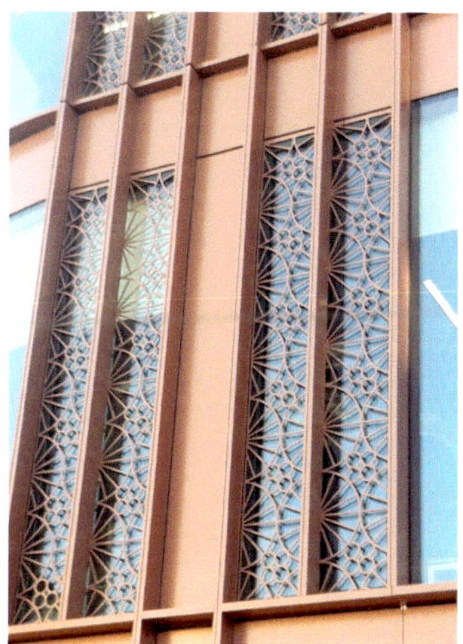

Above left: The Green Wall on the new car park at The Forum.

Above right: Panels at The Forum inspired by the Cloisters at Gloucester Cathedral.

Quirky Stories

Saddam the Pigeon

In 1996, a pigeon named Saddam was responsible for a project to replace the windows in a Gloucester tower block not being completed. Retired civil servant Marcia Sheldon-Jones was concerned that the work to install new double-glazed windows in her flat at Clapham Court in Kingsholm would upset Saddam, who she had adopted and named after the Iraqi dictator Saddam Hussein, along with a second pigeon called Redring. Mrs Sheldon-Jones reared Saddam from an egg in a nest box on her balcony and 'would talk to him all day long'.

Some of her neighbours petitioned the City Council, who at the time owned the building, complaining that it was being 'held to ransom by two pet pigeons'.

Saddam disappeared in 1998, leaving Mrs Sheldon-Jones 'heartbroken'. Mrs Sheldon-Jones placed an advert in the 'Lost & Found' section of *The Citizen* newspaper and offered a reward, but to no avail. The windows were eventually replaced.

Mortar This than Meets the Eye

The bomb squad was called to Gloucestershire Royal Hospital in the city in December 2021 after a patient was admitted with a mortar shell stuck up his bottom.

Troops from the 11 Explosive Ordnance Disposal Regiment rushed to the hospital after being notified by police 'that a patient had presented with a munition in his rectum'.

The man was a military enthusiast who found the shell while clearing out at home, but somehow 'tripped' and fell onto the 57-mm piece of army ordnance that landed him in hospital, according to a report in *The Sun*.

These mortar rounds were used by the Royal Artillery in the Second World War as anti-tank ammunition and were also later used by British tanks in North Africa.

A source told *The Sun*: 'The guy said he found the shell when he was having a clear out of his stuff.' He said he put it on the floor then he slipped and fell on it – and it went up his a***.'

The patient was released from hospital and was expected to make a full recovery, as long as he avoids a recurrence!

Jewellery Thief

I don't know what it is with people in Gloucester putting things up their behind, but in 2015 a thief stole a ring from Truscott's jewellers in College Court, near

Gloucester Cathedral, hiding it up his bum. He ran off, pursued by shop owner Ivan Taylor, who was in his seventies at the time, shouting 'stop thief!'

The thief hadn't bargained that a female rugby player was close by, who responded to Mr Taylor's plea and rugby tackled the thief to the ground and sat on him until the police arrived.

The New Inn

The New Inn, in Northgate Street, has had a few high-profile guests over the years, including Queen Juliana of the Netherlands, George Bernard Shaw and Charles Rolls of Rolls-Royce fame.

Mr Rolls stayed at the inn when the brakes on his car failed while he was coming down the very steep Birdlip Hill. He decided to stay the night in Gloucester before completing his journey home to Monmouthshire the next day.

The next morning his repaired car was waiting for him in the courtyard. Mr Rolls started the engine with the starting handle, but the car had been left in gear and it sprang forward, giving him the indignity of being run over by his own car!

In the second half of the eighteenth century, the inn was a base for travelling shows as they passed through the area. Some of the attractions included 'a two

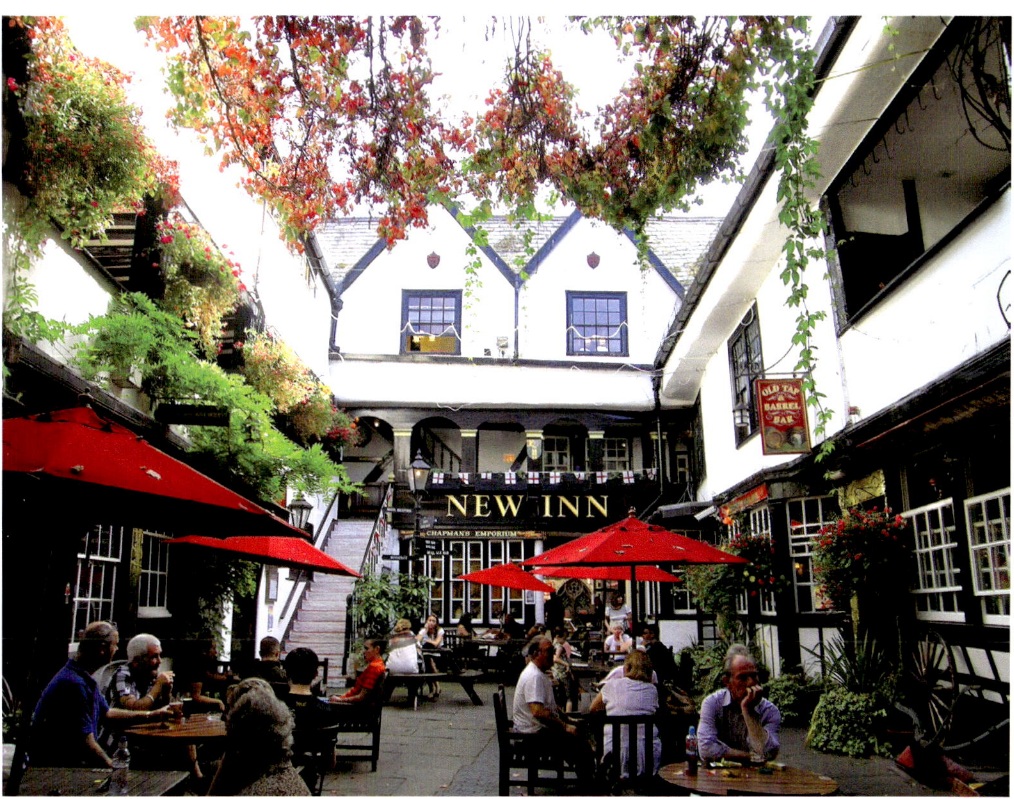

The New Inn. (Colin Organ)

foot ten inch midget which had the stage name of the "Corsican Fairy", a life-size waxwork Royal family, a mermaid supposedly netted off the coast of Mexico and a collection of wild animals, including leopards, lions, llamas, tigers and hyenas'.

Gandhi's Spectacles

A pair of Mahatma Gandhi's distinctive round steel-rimmed spectacles, bought from H. Cannam opticians at 23 St Aldate Street in Gloucester, were auctioned in 2012. The auction, which took place at Ludlow Racecourse, had put a guide price of £10,000 on the spectacles but the bidding reached £34,000. The glasses were bought by Gandhi when he was a student in England in the 1890s.

Gloucester's Heaviest Baby

Believed to be the largest baby ever born naturally in the UK, weighing 15lb 7oz, was George King, born at Gloucestershire Royal Hospital in Gloucester in February 2013.

George is only Britain's second biggest baby. The heaviest baby ever born in the UK was 15lb 8oz Guy Carr, from Barrow-in-Furness, Cumbria, in 1992.

Celebrating Gloucester

A Costume for Gloucester

A unique costume created by the local community was unveiled as part of the Gloucester Day parade in September 2023.

More than 100 people, including members of community groups and other partner organisations, worked to embroider the costume. The costume was designed by local costumier Katie Taylor and community artist Jo Teague to showcase the city's heritage and shows different parts of the city's history in each embroidered section.

Its creation was organised by local cultural organisation Voices Gloucester in collaboration with Gloucester Cathedral. In the parade it was worn by Voices Gloucester ambassador Tia Callum.

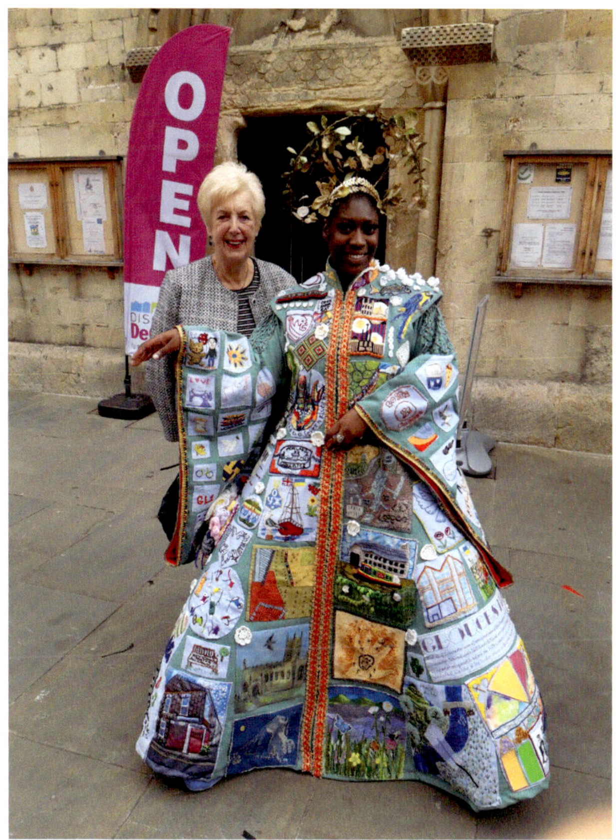

Tia Callum, wearing the Gloucester Costume, with Cllr Pam Tracey.

The Gloucester Rose

The 'City of Gloucester Rose' was created for the city by John Sanday (Roses) Ltd, based in Almondsbury, in 1969. The colour 'saffron yellow, shaded gold' was chosen in 1968 by Alderman Ken Hyett, then Mayor of Gloucester. The rose was officially launched on 24 November 1970 and planted at Gloucester Park. It was then sold commercially throughout the 1970s but has not been on sale since 1995 and was thought to have been lost.

The rose then fell out of fashion until 1998 when *The Citizen* newspaper, looking for ways to celebrate the millennium, decided to find specimens from which to propagate new plants. The project was a great success. 500 plants were raised, some planted at Gloucester Park and others at Gloucestershire Royal Hospital, whilst the rest were sold to people who felt nostalgic about the city.

A search for the rose was launched by Caroline Meller from the Gloucester Local History Society. Following months of searching, with the help of Radio Gloucestershire, in 2015 the rose was found in gardens in the Abbeydale, Tuffley and Barnwood areas of Gloucester.

Gloucester Events

Gloucester Goes Retro

People in Gloucester love dressing up and they love a bit of nostalgia, which accounts for the popularity of the Gloucester Goes Retro event. It takes place every August bank holiday Saturday and was founded by the late Colin Organ, who at the time was a city councillor.

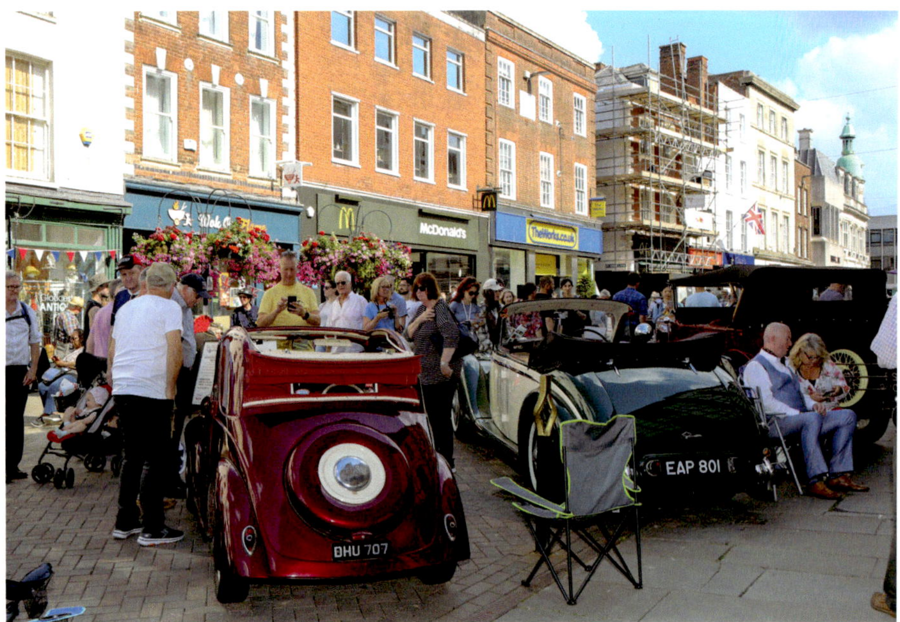

The city centre streets packed with vintage cars for Gloucester Goes Retro.

The city centre streets, and in more recent years Gloucester Docks, are divided into different eras and filled with classic cars, activities and characters. Hundreds of people dress up in the clothing from past eras, with a particular penchant for the 1950s.

Some of the vehicles on display have included a replica of James Bond's Aston Martin, a *Back to the Future* Delorean, a *Ghostbusters* ECTO1 and some American sheriffs' vehicles. For the younger generation, there has been a converted Lambretta made into a miniature Postman Pat van and a mini-Biggles bi-plane.

For a number of years stars from the TV sitcom *'Allo, 'Allo!* were part of the event, with Lieutenant Gruber (Guy Siner), Yvette (Vikki Michelle), Helga (Kim Hartman) and Herr Flick (Richard Gibson) walking around the city centre streets. They regularly got stopped by people at the event who would say, 'You don't half look like the real ones!'

They hit the national headlines in 2018 for being the first time that the cast had got together for twenty-six years.

One of the groups to take part in the event are the Gloucestershire Troopers. Gloucestershire Troopers was formed by three friends back in 2012 as a way of keeping in touch with each other. They fund their own screen-accurate costumes and travelling costs in order to attend small events in the local area. The group has grown year after year and now has over fifty costumed members from around Gloucestershire and surrounding areas and a few from a little further afield.

A few eyebrows were raised when a photo was posted on social media showing the Stormtroopers appearing to assist the police with an incident outside Gloucester's city centre branch of KFC.

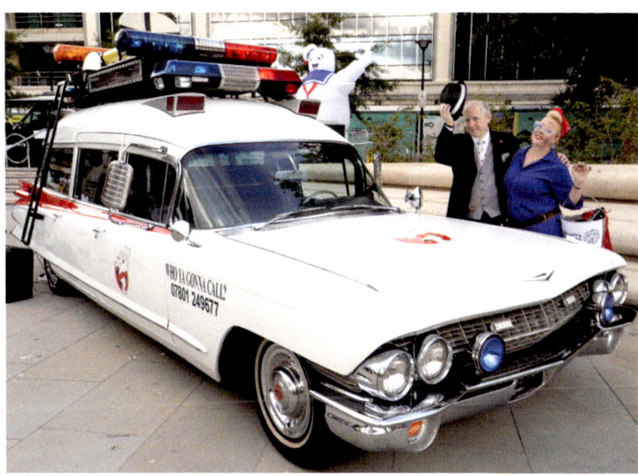

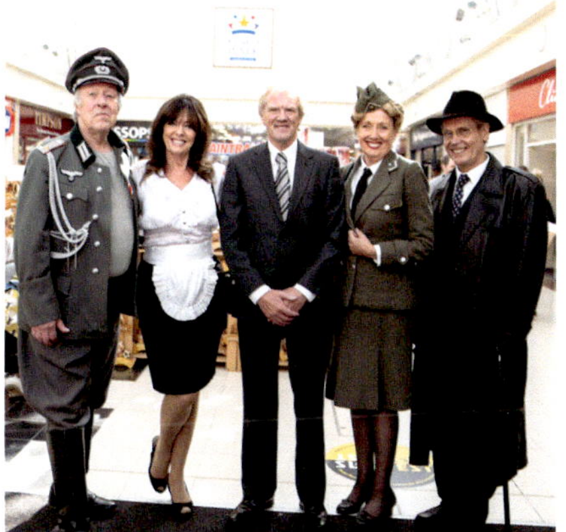

Above left: The Ghostbusters car. (Paul Nicholls)

Above right: Colin Organ with some of the cast of *'Allo, 'Allo!*

Gloucester Legends and Stories
Humpty Dumpty

The ever-popular nursery rhyme Humpty Dumpty may have its origins in the Siege of Gloucester of 1643. It was suggested that the nursery rhyme originated from a siege engine (more commonly known as catapult) used during the siege. However, other theories link the nursery rhyme to Colchester in Essex, as it's thought to be the name of a cannon that was used in the city during the English Civil War.

So the story goes, it was mounted on the walls of Llanthony Secunda Priory where the Royalist forces were encamped during the siege. It was apparently named (disparagingly) after a famously rotund MP of the day. As the artillerymen trained their sights on Gloucester's cathedral, the cannon misfired. Another assertion was that Humpty Dumpty was a 'tortoise' siege engine that featured a series of covered bridges to enable King Charles I's men to cross the defensive ditch and scale the city walls.

Some historians are a bit sniffy about whether Gloucester should be promoting this connection given that its origins are uncertain. Most people prefer not to let the facts (or the lack of them) get in the way of a good story.

At a special service on Gloucester Day, held at St Mary de Crypt church, a special 'Ode to a Siege Engine' is sung by Churchwarden Peter Gould in an adapted version of Humpty Dumpty which includes reference to something topical. This has ranged from the COVID-19 pandemic to the bizarre proposal by the Boundary Commission in 2014 to transfer the city centre Westgate Ward (which includes the cathedral and the Docks) to the Forest of Dean Parliamentary constituency. The relevant verse is reproduced below:

> This sad encounter with the city of Gloucester,
> Not unlike that of Doctor Foster,
> Serves us well in pursuit of the people's best fate,
> When under siege from those who would partition Westgate;
> Remember Humpty Dumpty who sat on our wall,
> That Humpty Dumpty who had a great fall.

Another memorable example was when, in 2019, the ode paid tribute to Town Crier Alan Myatt, the mastermind behind Gloucester Day. The verse went as follows:

> Worthy of mention is that noble Town Crier Alan Myatt,
> Whose voice cannot be described even remotely as 'quiet',
> Who, like Colonel Massey, that Civil War leader of fame,
> Has brought people together in defence of the city's good name,
> But who, unlike that self-same Massey,
> Would never be able to escape from a gaol by climbing up through a chimney.
> (Massey did; look it up)

Doctor Foster

> Doctor Foster
> Went to Gloucester
> In a shower of rain
> He stepped in a puddle
> Right up to his middle
> And never went there again

More obviously linked to Gloucester is the nursery rhyme Doctor Foster. Although it was first published in 1844, it is believed that the origins of this rhyme date back over 700 years, to the time of King Edward I. The nursery rhyme is thought to refer to a time when the king arrived in Gloucester during a storm and fell into a deep, muddy puddle. Humiliated by the experience, King Edward I vowed never to return to Gloucester.

Surprisingly for such a well-known rhyme, the only reference in the city to Doctor Foster is a pub in the Docks bearing his name. Perhaps it's because people don't want to be reminded of what could be seen as a negative story about the King vowing never to return …

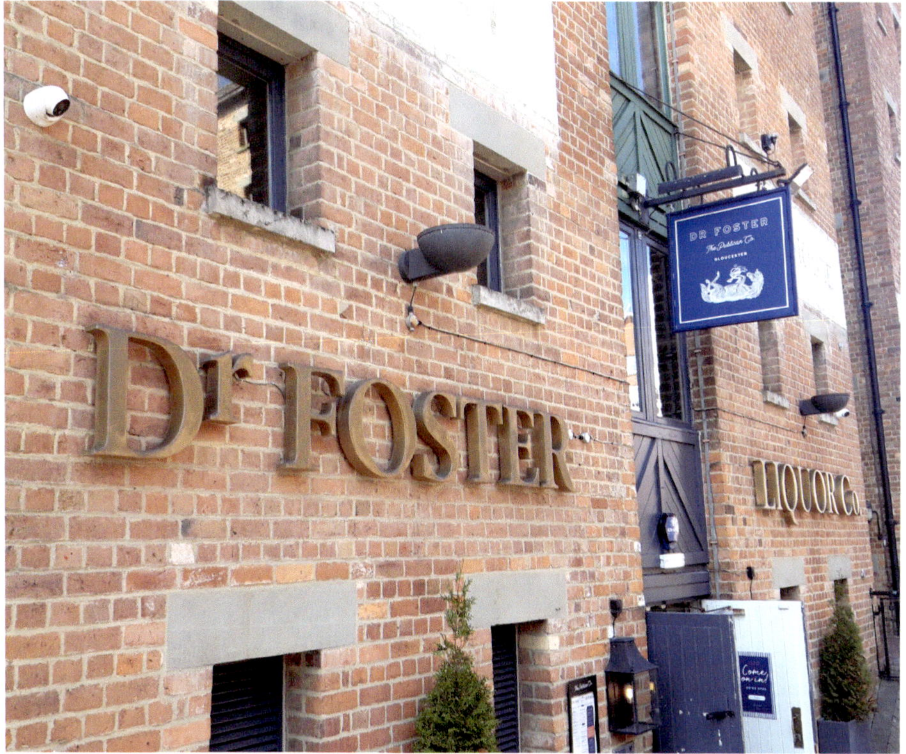

The Doctor Foster pub at the Docks.

The Tailor of Gloucester

Beatrix Potter's 'Tailor of Gloucester' is probably the most famous story involving Gloucester.

It involves the story of a tailor who is making a waistcoat for the Mayor of Gloucester to wear at his wedding which was to take place on Christmas Day. The waistcoat is finished off by mice. The story is based on a real-life tailor, John Prichard, who had his shop at 45 Westgate Street. Beatrix Potter, however, thought that 9 College Court was a more attractive building, so she sketched it instead. 9 College Court is now where the House of the Tailor of Gloucester shop and museum is based.

45 Westgate Street is now part of The Sword Inn and is an interesting building in itself in that the windows on the third floor are false with glazing and bars painted on the wall! For a while it was called The Tailor's House to celebrate the link with the story.

There is now a set of ten brass plaques depicting mice from The Tailor of Gloucester hidden along Westgate Street. Beatrix Potter has many dedicated fans. One made a special trip to Gloucester to visit the MT Moon tattoo parlour, just opposite the House of the Tailor of Gloucester, to get a Jemima Puddle-duck tattoo done. This was to add to the one she already had of Peter Rabbit!

There was a Tailor of Gloucester clock in the Eastgate Shopping Centre by the entrance to the Indoor Market, which was a popular feature, until it was

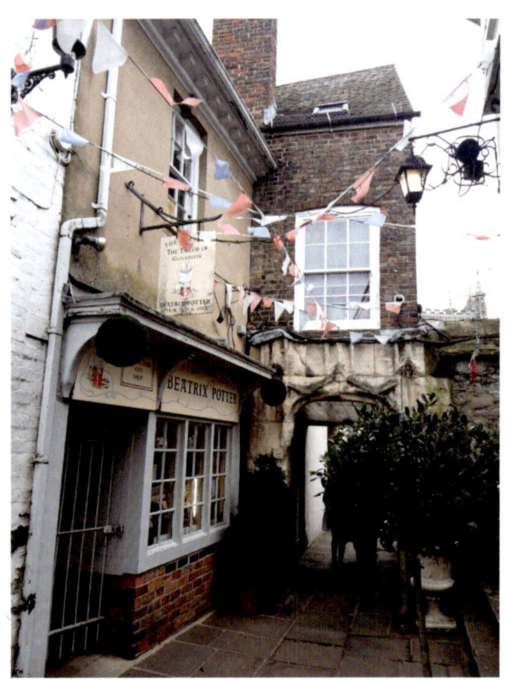

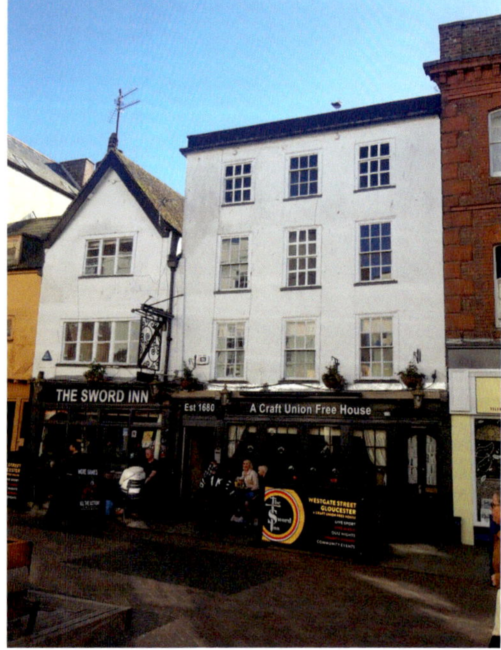

Above left: The House of the Tailor of Gloucester.

Above right: 45 Westgate Street with its false windows

removed in 2013. It was said at the time that the cost of its frequent breakdowns became too much for the centre management. Nonetheless its removal is still much lamented. It was given to the Pied Piper Appeal with the idea of installing it at the Children's Hospital at Gloucestershire Royal. Despite years of negotiations, agreement couldn't be reached with the NHS and the clock was broken up, with the various characters refurbished by Severn Signs of Innsworth and given to various special schools around the county, including Milestone School in Longlevens, in 2021. The various pieces were collected in and brought back to the Eastgate Shopping Centre to go on display in April 2025.

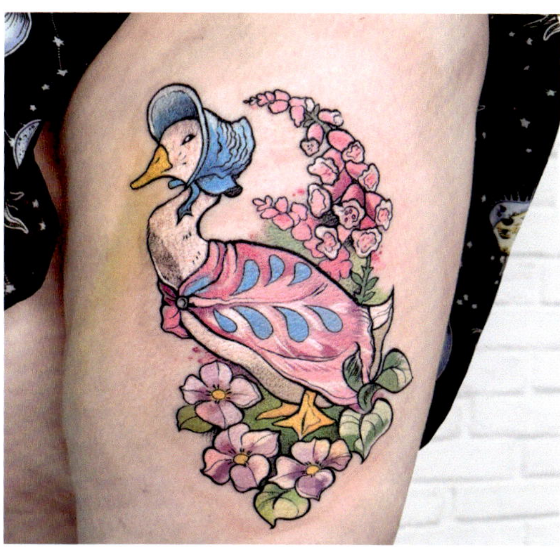

Right: A tattoo of Jemima Puddle-duck. (Mt. Moon Tattoo)

Below: The 'other' Tailor of Gloucester, Nazer Radae.

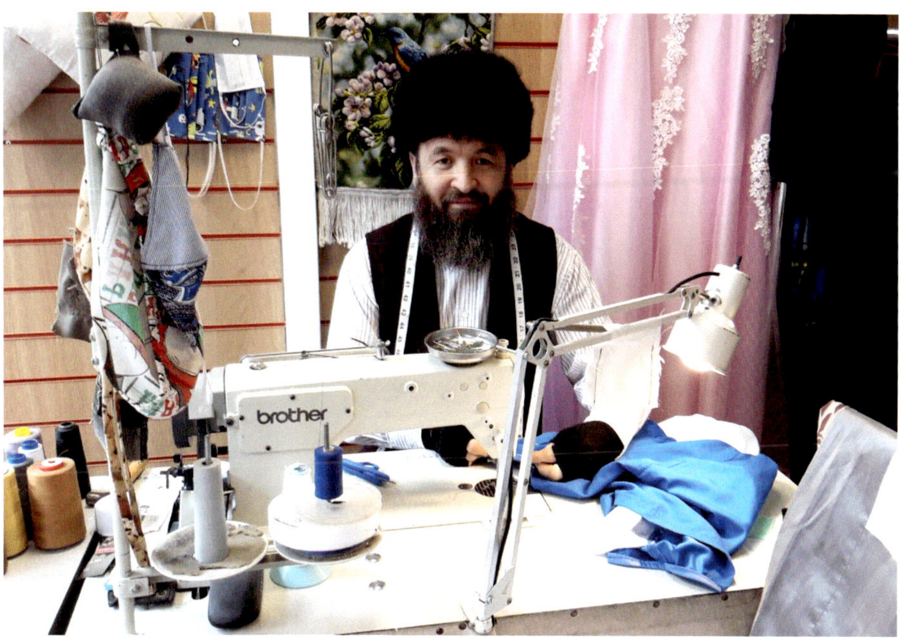

One point of potential confusion is that Southgate Street is also home to the 'Tailor of Gloster' (note the slightly different spelling). This is a shop for clothing repairs and alterations run by Afghan Nazer Radae. Some customers turn up at his shop looking for Beatrix Potter memorabilia and some arrive at College Court expecting to drop off clothing for repair.

Gloucester has something of a history of tailoring. It was home to the Gloucester Shirt Company in Magdala Road for many years. That tradition continues today with Turnbull & Asser being based in Quedgeley. Someone else who can lay claim to the title of modern-day Tailor of Gloucester is Emma Willis, who runs her eponymous shirt-making business from the historic Bearland House in the city centre. Customers for her made-to-measure shirts include King Charles III and James Bond star Daniel Craig.

Priday's Mill Law Case

The building is notable for the 1854 Hadley v Baxendale landmark legal case which established the foreseeability test for consequential damages for breach of contract, which is used internationally, particularly in the US. The case centred on a broken steam engine shaft at the mill. The shaft could only be repaired in Greenwich, some 125 miles away. The owners of the City Flour Mill, Joseph and Jonah Hadley, hired a moving company, Pickfords, which was operated by Baxendale. For an unexplained reason, the shaft went astray and ended up on a canal boat instead of a train and took several days to reach Greenwich, during which time the mill lay idle. They sued Pickfords for the money they lost while it sat idle. The Court ruled that Pickfords could not be held liable for that level of damages as they did not necessarily know that the mill could not function without it – hence the 'foreseeability' test for contract breaches: you cannot be held liable for losses you could not have reasonably anticipated.

Gloucester Rugby

Rugby, and in particular the support of the city's Premiership team, is a big part of life in Gloucester. People can be seen wearing Gloucester Rugby clothing at any time – something which club captain Lewis Ludlow found surprising, but in a good way, when he moved to the city.

On match days, the city centre is a sea of cherry and white shirts as fans eat, drink and shop before taking the short walk to the Kingsholm stadium. Whilst football fans seem to want to wear the latest version of the shirt, some Gloucester fans view wearing the oldest one possible as a badge of honour!

Supporters, particularly in Kingsholm's famous Shed, can be very vocal. When opposition players make a mistake, they are greeted with 'eeyore' donkey noises and when the referee makes a decision that the home crowd doesn't like there are usually chants of 'You don't know what you're doing.'

Danny Sparkes has been going to Gloucester rugby matches for over thirty years and has always watched from The Shed. Like many 'Shedheads', he would

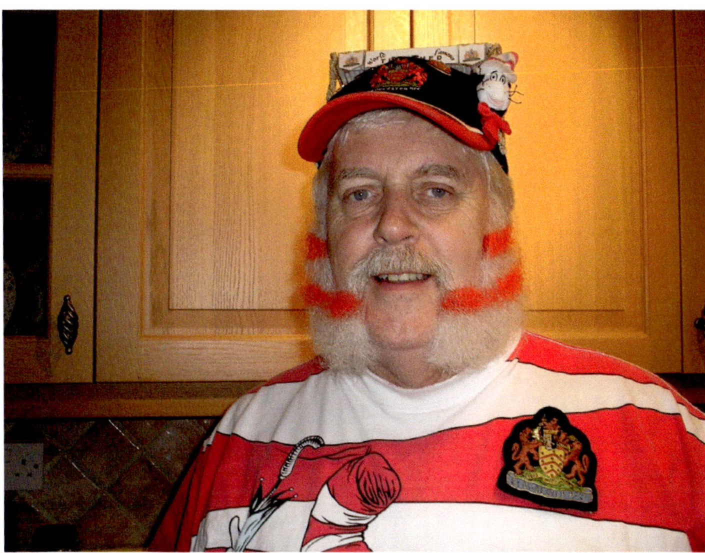

Danny Sparkes with his cherry and white sideburns.

get to the Kingsholm stadium up to two hours before kick-off to secure his favourite vantage point (although the club more recently delayed opening the turnstiles until an hour and a half before kick-off). He often attracts attention because of his special 'Shed' cap. Danny says it means that 'no matter where he is', he's 'always in The Shed'. One year, for a trip to Paris to watch Gloucester play in a European match, he grew an enormous pair of sideburns which he turned to cherry and white stripes. Lots of supporters pulled them to see if they were real!

In 2018, when Gloucester Rugby changed their logo, they offered to pay for fans with tattoos of their old crest to have inkings of the new club logo to ease any ill feeling about the rebranding.

In 2017, fan Shoshone Bishop became the proud owner of an incredibly detailed (and big) tattoo of Welsh international hooker Richard Hibbard. The eighteen-year-old care assistant from Coney Hill sat through four hours under the needle at the Alzone tattoo parlour in Eastgate Street to get the image of the player on her calf. Gloucester has its own rugby song, 'We are the Gloucester Boys'. The words are reproduced below:

> We are from Glo'ster, the pride of the west,
> Some of the lads and some of the best,
> We are respected wherever we go,
> Where we come from nobody knows.
> They call us the pride of the ladies, the ladies;
> We spend all our wages, our wages, our wages;
> We are respected wherever we go.
> We are the Glo'ster boys.

Maggie dear, pint of beer a woodbine and a match,
A tuppence ha'penny stick of rock,
we're off to the rugby match.
To see ol' Glo'ster score a try,
the best try in the land.
We are the Glo'ster boys!

We are the Glo'ster boys, we are the Glo'ster boys;
We know our manners, we spend our tanners,
We are respected wherever we may go.
And when you're walking down the Kingsholm Road,
Doors and windows open wide.
You can here the people shout
"Put them bloody Woodbines out!"
'Cause we are the Glo'ster boys

Some versions use Bristol Road rather than Kingsholm Road, with fear of setting fire to the Morelands match factory being the reason for being told to put the Woodbines out!

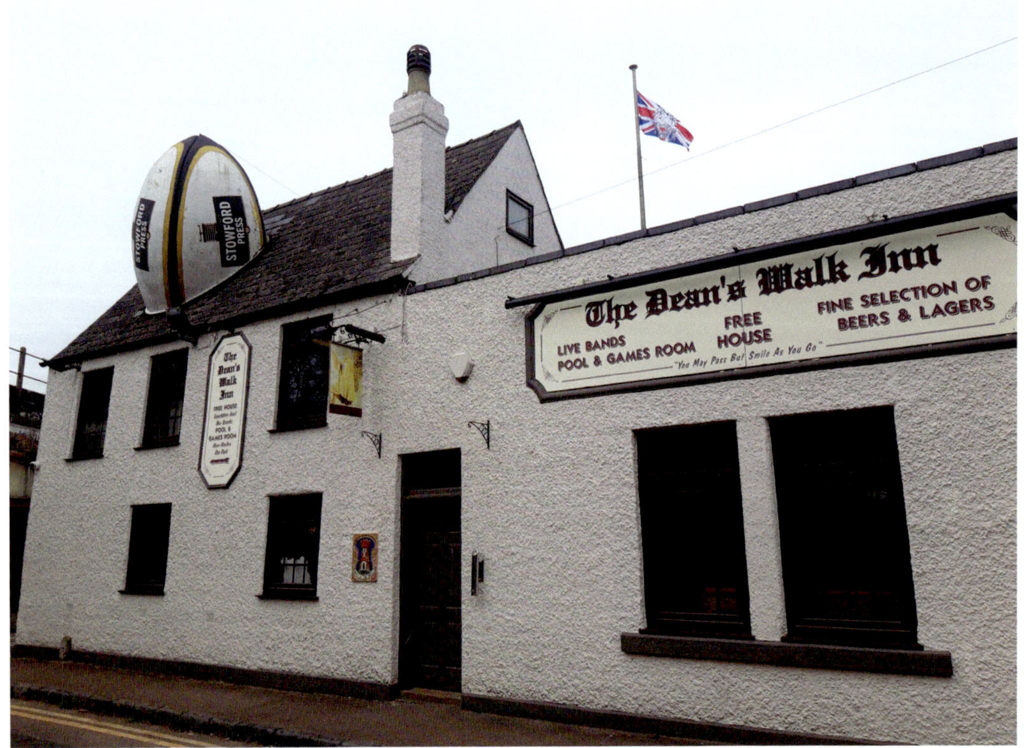

The Dean's Walk Inn, complete with a rugby ball sticking out of the roof.

It is said that after Gloucester won the first National Knockout Competition in 1972, the sounds of 'We are the Gloucester Boys' echoed round the Palace of Westminster after a celebration dinner organised by the city's then MP, Sally Oppenheim.

These days Gloucester Rugby have a slightly different song which the players sing in the changing rooms (recorded and shared on social media, of course!) after winning a match, which is 'We are the boys from Gloucester', lyrics as follows:

> We are the boys from Gloucester, this is true, this is true.
> And we really have enjoyed beating you, beating you.
> It was really nice to meet you, even better 'cause we beat you.
> Why don't you join us for a beer or two, beer or two!
> Singing aye aye yippee yippee aye, Gloucester!
> Singing aye aye yippee, aye aye yippee, aye aye yippee yippee aye Gloucester!

New player recruits to Gloucester Rugby have to go through a quirky initiation known as the 'Milk Challenge'. According to the rules, if players can drink 8 pints of milk in twenty minutes without being sick, they pass the test. If they fail to do that, then their hair gets shaved off.

Many of the pubs around Kingsholm, perhaps unsurprisingly, have a rugby theme. Teague's Bar, formerly The White Hart, was described by a *Guardian* journalist as 'the most rugby-crazed pub in the country's most rugby-crazed city'. Just a short walk away is the Kingsholm Inn, known by locals as 'The Jockey' – which can sometimes result in people not familiar with the area spending time searching for a pub with a sign saying 'The Jockey', until recently there hasn't been one.

The nearby Deans Walk Inn went one step further to show their rugby-supporting credentials and has a huge rugby ball protruding from the roof. The then landlord, Bruce Drake, installed the feature in 1992. The pub's sign shows the former Dean of Gloucester, Nicholas Bury, who served as Dean from 1997 to 2010.

The Red Ants

In the 1990s, Spartans Rugby Club played a Combination Cup match in their traditional red shirts. A report of the game in *The Citizen* newspaper stated that the side were a much smaller team than the opposition but beat them and 'were all over them like a swarm of red ants'.

The club then made it through to the final at Kingsholm and the lads in charge of the scoreboard put up 'Red Ants' instead of Spartans. This prompted one of the players to have a red ant tattooed on his bum. Within days this was followed by several other players and within weeks 90 per cent of the players had the tattoo.

This custom has been followed ever since although not by so many as previously.

Civic Gloucester

The Mayor and Sheriff

The civic offices of mayor and sheriff have been part of life in Gloucester for hundreds of years. The city still celebrates the civic traditions involved with these roles and, along with the rest of the City Council, the mayor and sheriff can regularly be seen processing through the city centre streets on occasions like the Annual Civic Service and Remembrance Sunday. They are accompanied by a sword bearer and four ceremonial officers carrying gold maces.

The mayor's chain and badge were purchased by subscription at a cost of £220 and presented to the Corporation in April 1870. In 1932/3 the mayor of the day, W. L. Edwards, had the horseshoes reversed. They had been mounted with their points downwards, and he had them replaced points upwards. This reflects the modern idea that the luck of horseshoes is trapped within the bowl formed by the bow of the shoe. Theodore Hannam-Clarke became mayor for 1933/4 and remembered the chain as his father had worn it – with the shoes pointing down. After a year-long debate, which attracted national media attention, and the discovery that there had been no council approval for the action, the chain was restored to its original form!

In 2003, then Mayor Pam Tracey was distressed to find one of the red enamel lions of the city crest had fallen off the pendant. After an article was published in *The Citizen* newspaper, it was found in the gutter outside the GL1 Leisure Centre. After being repaired, a replica pendant was created at a cost believed to be £8,000 and the original pendant is now safely located as part of the civic display cabinets at the City Council's North Warehouse building.

The mayor is seen as an office of dignity and is usually above the party political fray. Occasionally, the mayor can get dragged into controversy. For instance, decades when Miss Gloucester became pregnant, a councillor claimed the mayor was the father. He wasn't and successfully sued for slander.

Many towns and cities have a mayor but only fifteen places in England and Wales, including Gloucester, have a sheriff. The sheriff used to have a law enforcement role and presided over the courts, but these days it is just a ceremonial position.

The sheriff's chain and badge of office were presented to Mr Henry Jeffs by his brother Freemasons when he was sheriff in 1883. Mr Jeffs gave the chain to the Corporation at the end of his term of office for the use of future sheriffs. Mr Jeffs is buried in the churchyard at St Swithins, Hempsted.

The Gloucester Services M5 motorway services station sells a 'Sheriff's sausage roll' made by Cinderhill Farm in the Forest of Dean.

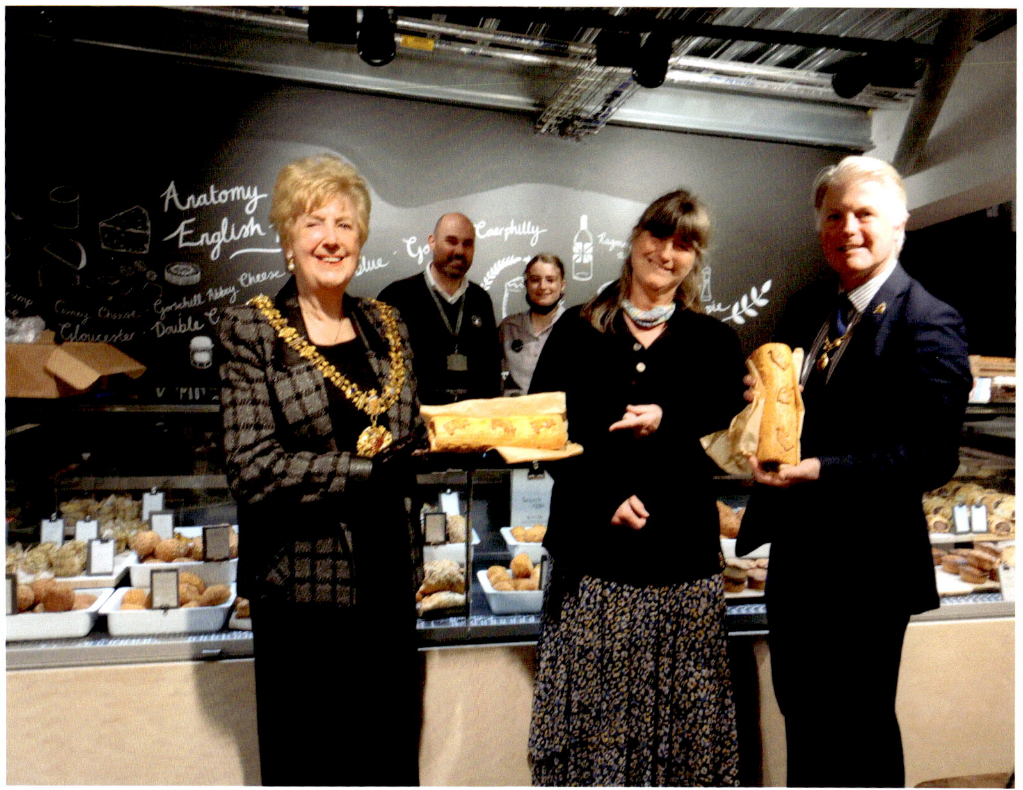

Sheriff Pam Tracey and consort Paul James receive a Sheriff's sausage roll from Deborah Flint at the M5 Gloucester Services. (Gloucestershire Gateway Trust)

In March 2025, a project was announced to restore an old watermill off Abbeymead Avenue known as the 'Sheriff's Mill' because it was owned by a former Sheriff of Gloucester.

Richard III

King Richard III was the Duke of Gloucester. He wasn't believed to have visited the city very often, unlike Prince Richard, the current Duke of Gloucester, who is a regular visitor and great supporter of the city that bears his name.

After Richard III's body was discovered under a car park in Leicester in 2012, a facial reconstruction was created by the University of Dundee and went on display in the Museum of Gloucester in 2014. The exhibition coincided with a visit to the city by the Duke and Mayor of Gloucester at the time, Chris Chatterton, who showed it to the royal visitor with the words 'Prince Richard, meet Prince Richard.'

International Links

US Connections

Gloucester can boast a number of connections with the USA. Some are well known, such as John Stafford Smith, the son of a Gloucester Cathedral organist, writing the music for what would become the US national anthem, the Star-Spangled Banner.

Slightly less well known is the fact that Button Gwinnett, who was born at Down Hatherley just outside Gloucester, was the second signatory to the US Declaration of Independence in 1776. His father was the vicar of Down Hatherley but was also the curate at St Nicholas Church in Westgate Street for a while and, during that time, the family lived in College Green in the cathedral precincts.

Button was believed to have attended the College School (now known as The King's School) but the records for that time are missing. He went off to America,

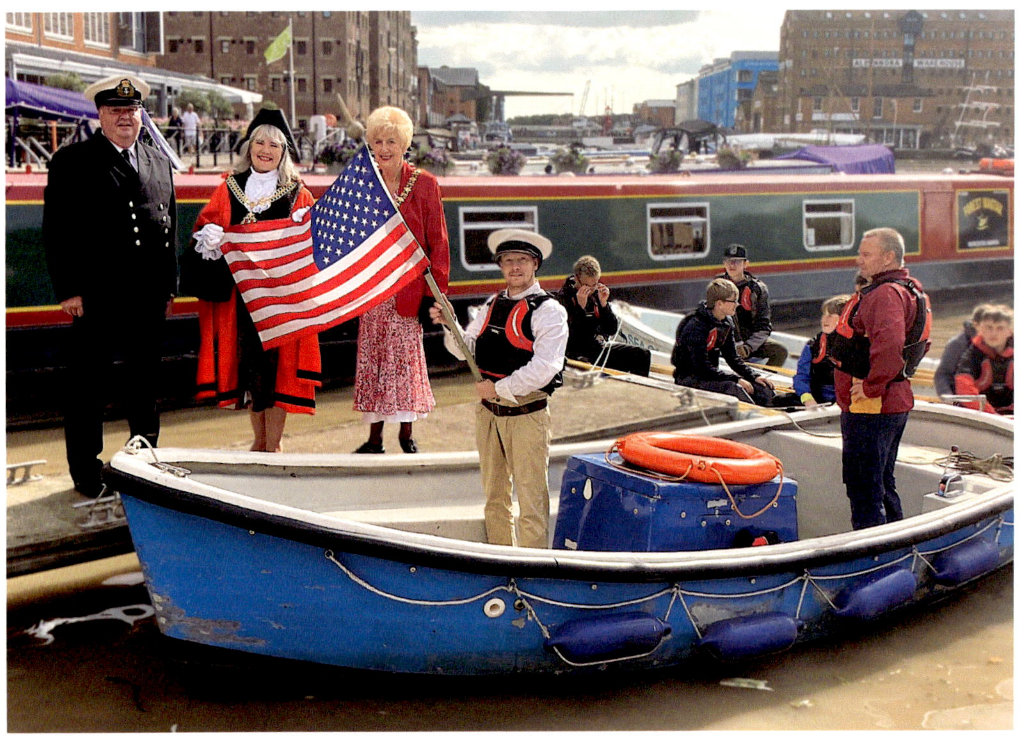

The re-enactment of Captain Howard Blackburn arriving at Gloucester Docks. (Ross Campbell)

became a plantation owner and later Governor of Georgia – in which role he signed the declaration. He came to an inconspicuous end when challenged to a duel by his long-time rival Lachlan McIntosh. He was shot in the leg, which went gangrenous and this ultimately killed him.

The character Button Gwinnett features in the Fallout 3 and Fallout 4 role-playing games played on the Xbox and PlayStation.

Another US connection is George Whitefield, who was born at the Bell Hotel in Southgate Street, attended The Crypt School and preached his first sermon in St Mary de Crypt church. The pulpit he used is still in the church. He travelled to the USA and helped to spread the 'Great Awakening', preaching to millions of people. While in the US, he established the Bethesda orphanage in Georgia. One person who spent time there as a young person was a certain Lachlan McIntosh!

A fascinating story linking Gloucester to its US namesake is that of Captain Howard Blackburn. He arrived in Gloucester Docks on Saturday 19 August 1899, sixty-one days after leaving the fishing port of Gloucester, Massachusetts. His voyage was all the more remarkable as he had lost all of his fingers and some of his toes to frostbite on an earlier expedition.

In August 2024, to mark the 125th anniversary of the voyage, Gloucester Sea Cadets rowed into the main basin at Gloucester Docks with former councillor Gordon Taylor as Captain Blackburn, to be greeted by the Mayor of Gloucester Councillor Lorraine Campbell, Sheriff Councillor Pam Tracey and Town Crier Alan Myatt on the North Quay.

In more recent years, it has been revealed that former US President George W. Bush was a descendant of Charles Hoare, who was Sheriff of Gloucester in 1634, although 'Dubya' hasn't publicly acknowledged the connection, let alone visited the city.

Even Donald Trump himself can claim a Gloucester connection, albeit a pretty tenuous one. In 2017, it was reported that a Cadillac limousine formerly owned by Trump was for sale through a Gloucester-based car dealer for a cool £50,000.

Twin Cities and the Plastic Statue

Gloucester is twinned with Metz in France, Trier in Germany, Gouda in the Netherlands and St Ann in Jamaica. These days the links only involve the exchange of Christmas cards and perhaps the occasional visit by the mayor (at their own expense). Gloucester has roads named after all of these places.

Trier's most famous son is the revolutionary socialist philosopher Karl Marx. In 2013, to celebrate the 195th anniversary of his birth, the city produced 500 red plastic statues of him. One was later given to a member of the Gloslinks twinning organisation to pass to the civic leaders in Gloucester. While waiting for an answer from the City Council about what should happen to it, it was kept in the gentleman in question's garden in Tuffley Avenue – rather like a garden gnome!

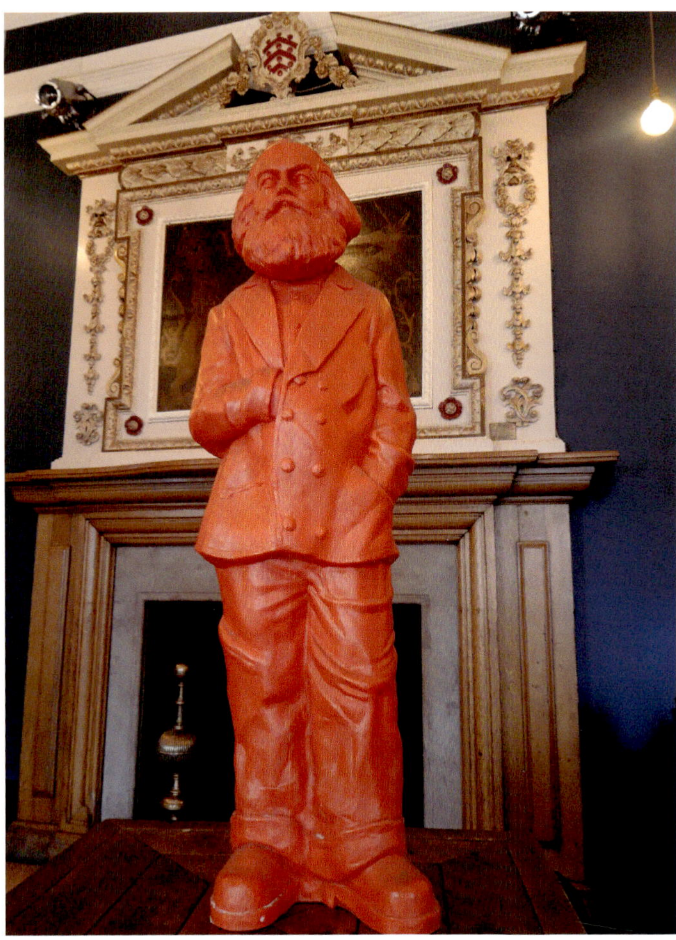

The red plastic statue of Karl Marx at Gloucester Guildhall.

A place was found for it in the city's Guildhall, but its fate hit the national media after the City Council Leader at the time (the author) gave a tongue-in-cheek quote about why it shouldn't be put anywhere more prominent.

Paju Walk

As well as its town cities, Gloucester has a link with Paju City in South Korea, after signing a 'Memorandum of Understanding' in 2014. This friendship has its roots in the Korean War (1950–53) when the Gloucestershire Regiment played a vital role in the Battle of Imjin River, holding out against a much larger Chinese Army, allowing time for United Nations reinforcements to arrive – something for which the South Koreans remain enormously grateful.

As a sign of this relationship, the walkway alongside the Victoria Basin in Gloucester Docks is named Paju Walk. Paju has been very generous to Gloucester, including donating a large sum of money to the Soldiers of Gloucestershire Museum to create a Korean War gallery.

Gloucester's World Records

Hal Bagwell

Hal Bagwell was a record-breaking lightweight boxer who held the British record of being unbeaten in the ring for ten years and three months. The claim, made in the Guinness Book of Records, attributed to him the world record for the most consecutive professional boxing contests without a loss (an amazing 183 fights between 10 August 1938 and 29 November 1948 when he lost to Morry Jones of Liverpool on points), although Hal himself modestly refuted this, saying it was closer to eighty-three. The statistic was disputed due to a lack of proof and was later removed from the record books.

Dick Sheppard

'Daredevil' Dick Sheppard was a stunt driver and showman who once held the record for having the most entries in the Guinness Book of Records. The three times married father of nine, who also had a stepdaughter, died in 2021, aged ninety.

He boasted that he had wrecked 2,003 cars, appeared in 500 films, including the iconic Michael Caine classic *The Italian Job* and James Bond's *Thunderball* and *Diamonds Are Forever*, and held eighteen world records during his career. He said he regarded his greatest achievements as being top points winner in stock car racing for four consecutive seasons, his numerous world records and writing a successful book about his exploits. He featured in the Guinness Book of Records every year from 1969 to 1996.

Alan Myatt

Town Crier Alan Myatt set two Guinness World Records – the loudest crier, recording a cry of 112.8 decibels, and the record for vocal endurance, issuing a one-hundred-word proclamation every fifteen minutes for a period of forty-eight hours.

Jamie McDonald

Jamie McDonald made the decision to attempt the world static cycling record, which stood at 224 hours and 24 minutes. He stepped off the exercise bike, set up within a marquee on the North Quay at Gloucester Docks, after pedalling for a Guinness World Record-breaking 268 hours – more than eleven days.

In 2023, he set a new record for travelling around the Seven Modern Wonders of the World in six days while raising money for charity. The trip consisted of thirteen flights, sixteen taxis, nine buses, four trains and one toboggan. He became the world record holder after completing the 22,856-mile (36,783 km) journey across nine countries in only six days.

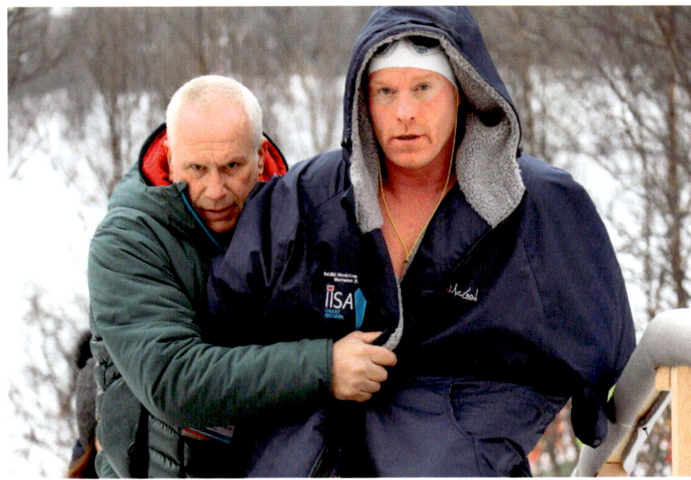

John Myatt
being supported
by Jon Coe
after swimming
in icy water.
(Colin Hill)

John Myatt and Other Swimmers

In 2018, Gloucester swimmers John Myatt and Mark Leighton completed the first two-man two-way English Channel relay swim (42 miles) in 22 hours, 49 minutes. The following year, at the age of forty-seven, John became Great Britain's 1 km age group ice swimming champion and won gold in the 45–49 age group 1 km race at the World Ice Swimming Championships in Murmansk, Russia (in 0°C water).

In 2020, he walked 91 miles along Hadrian's Wall in four days, dressed only in trunks and a Roman helmet, raising over £2,000 for armed forces charity Rugby for Heroes. In January 2024, he joined a five-man team for the first winter relay crossing of the English Channel, the earliest and coldest on record (7°C water, 1°C air).

Gloucestershire boasts a lively ice swimming community, hosting events like the British International Ice Swimming Championships at Sandford Parks Lido in Cheltenham. Sallie Cheung, sixty-nine, from Hucclecote, and Jonathan Coe, seventy-one, earned spots on Great Britain's team for the inaugural European Ice Swimming Championships in Romania in 2024. Coe had been British champion in his age group for the previous six years.

Andy Brown

Andy Brown, while playing for Widden Old Boys Rugby Club, got his name in the record books for the quickest try ever scored from kick-off, in either an amateur or professional game of rugby. The game was fortunately being filmed, so Andy rightfully claimed his record. At the time of writing, the record still stands at just eight seconds.